THESE FEW
ALSO PAID
A PRICE

2

ALSO BY G. MCLEOD BRYAN

Voices in the Wilderness:
Twentieth Century Prophets Speak to the New Millennium
(Mercer University Press, 1999)

Communities of Faith and Radical Discipleship (Editor)
(Mercer University Press, 1986)

Dissenter in the Baptist Southland:
Fifty Years in the Career of William Wallace Finlator
(Mercer University Press, 1985)

THESE FEW ALSO PAID A PRICE

SOUTHERN WHITES WHO FOUGHT FOR CIVIL RIGHTS

G. M^CLEOD BRYAN

MERCER UNIVERSITY PRESS 2001

Dedicated to
Colette Love
Who has taken her stand in today's world
and
Robert Chukinas

ISBN 0-86554-732-7
MUP/H549

© 2001 Mercer University Press
6316 Peake Road
Macon, Georgia 31210-3960
All rights reserved

First Edition.

Dust jacket design by Jim Burt of *Burt&Burt Studio*
Book Design by Marc A. Jolley

∞The paper used in this publication meets the minimum
requirements of American National Standard for Information Sciences—Permanence of Paper for Printed Library
Materials, ANSI Z39.48-1992.

Library of Congress Cataloging-in-Publication Data

CONTENTS

FOREWORD

Too much love
Too much love
Nothing kills a nigger like
Too much love
(Author unknown)

I can still remember first hearing the words to this song, even while
never quite fully knowing what they meant (the final interpre-
tation I leave up to you). I was young and pubescent then, a pre-
teen I think, struggling with the churning and incessant realities of
being a young Black male growing up in the nineteen-sixties
America. Those years were often torturous for me, living as it were
in the snow country of Minnesota. Now by "snow country," I am
not referring to the winter weather so much as the bone-chilling
reality of growing up in a blizzard of white hostility that was Anglo,
German, Irish, and especially Scandinavian in origin. Walking the
mean streets of our all-white neighborhood (with the lone
exception of our family) honed survival skills born out of the
crucible of the spirit. Not surprisingly, my questions, which were
fiercely insistent, always personal, and, at times, political, turned
out to be no different from those being raised by my Black kith
and kin everywhere across this land an, especially, in the deep
South. Why were white people so evil (and why did "respectable"
whites always fall silent on the subject of racism)? My spirit ached
within me. What had Black people done to deserve such
treatment? Were good white people just a myth? Did they exist?
Could they exist? Anywhere?

The twentieth century has come to a close. One hundred years
more have passed. The end of another millennium is upon us. Yet,
tragically, the defining problem of what has been called "America's
century" looms as the legacy of the next. As one of our nation's

greatest prophets, W.E.B. DuBois, wrote long ago in *The Souls of Black Folk*, the problem of the twentieth century would be "the relation of the darker to the lighter races of men in Asia and Africa, in America and the islands of the sea."[1] The capitulation of our nation to white racial privilege and advancement, the ongoing disparagement of her darker sisters and brothers is still the defining and divisive dilemma of our day. What, if any is out grounds for hope?

It is fitting to reflect if but for a moment on another honored phrase from an even earlier American century: "There are times which try men's [and women's] souls." So observed the colonial-era patriot Thomas Paine, who realized that race (among other things) threatened to undermine the noble experiment called democracy even before it began. Over the centuries indigenous peoples, joined by those of European, African, and Asian descent have played a decisive role in our country's long and painful odyssey toward "a more perfect union." We have struggled with one another, misunderstood one another, feared one another, violated one another, and on the rarest of occasions, loved one another.

It is fairly easy to contend, where race relations are concerned, that our nation is being more severely tried today than ever before. The White Citizen Council has been supplanted by latter-day White Nationalists. The Ku Klux Klan has been surpassed by the Christian Identity Movement. Neo-Nazis, Aryans, Skinheads and assorted other survivalist and militia groups dot the land. In the words of the noted poet Herbert Woodward martin: "Nothing has changed; we have slipped backward. A good deal has changed; we are moving forward."[2] Somewhere, in between these polar

---

[1] W. E. B. DuBois, *The Souls of Black Folk* (Greenwich CT: Fawcett Publications, 1961) 23.
[2] Herbert Woodward Martin, "The Dreamer has gone to Sleep," in *Black Issues in Higher Education* (June 3, 1993): 26-7.

assertions, these irreconcilable statements, these antithetical views, lies the truth about who we are and where we are going as a nation.

As symptomatic as these groups may be of our national woes, in point of fact we are now confronted with something far more perilous than the reality (and it is real) of racism resurgent. We are seeing what happens to a nation and its people when social progress is stalled, when democracy no longer expands, and transcendent possibilities wane. In the human order, as in other manifestations of nature, stasis is never an option. It is a simple truth: either we move forward or we die. This is what Martin Luther King, Jr. understood full well at the end of his triumphal and costly march from Selma to Montgomery in 1965 when he said, "We must keep going."

My dear brother and friend G. McLeod "Mac" Bryan has marshaled evidence from that great mid-twentieth century movement of souls in our land, chronicling the witness of more than a few whites who paid a price for believing in racial and human justice. In so doing, he serves to remind us that liberating lessons yet remain to be learned for all of us who hunger and thirst after righteousness in our own day and time. At various points along the way, from the 1950s until now, most whites (often otherwise deeply committed Christians) have never been sure how much they really wanted democracy expanded, if at all, and who would be the people deemed worthy to share in it if they did. Under divine indictment were the churches of white America, outposts of exclusion, practitioners of irresponsible piety, exemplars of the will to quarantine. Is it any wonder that the "God is dead" movement occurred at the height of the black-led justice-obsessed movement for freedom?

One generation removed, Mac Bryan's *These Few Also Paid A Price* vividly recounts that there were white persons who, despite their relative privilege and prosperity, were ready "to do justice and love mercy." These are they who were willing to learn from their black sisters and brothers something of the meaning of a

better country, who were inspired by visions of democracy un-
leashed, transformed by the raging fires in their own sprit, im-
mersed in the power of God so self-evidently at work. Regrettably,
one story we are not privileged to read in this volume belongs to
Mac himself (and his lovely life-companion Edna). I say this not to
embarrass him, but to emphasize the fact that for many he, too,
has been and continues to be a marvelous beacon of hope. Mac has
long traveled the lifeway we read about in these pages. In fine,
These Few profiles in courage, dignity, hope, and faith—the cloud
of witnesses includes Bob Zellner, Mary King, Virginia Durr,
David minter, Zev Aelony, and more—are rich and vital repository
of strength for our own twenty-first century movement toward the
beloved community. May we remember and never forget.

Dr. Alton B. Pollard, III
Director, and Associate Professor of
Religion and Culture
Program of Black Church Studies
Candler School of Theology
Emory University

PREFACE

These select whites from the South, because of their participation
in the civil rights movement, were threatened, ostracized, beaten,
arrested, and jailed. Their personal stories in this book tend to
emphasize the agonies, the fears, the feelings of rejection, and the
hurt of those few whites who took their stand alongside their black
brothers and sisters. However, there is another side to their story.
The price they paid was cheap when weighed against the gain that
accrued from their stance. Redemptive suffering was no longer an
academic term; they witnessed it being born in a people before it
became a theoretical alternative. Non-violent action suddenly became a reality; their black brothers and sisters underwent disci-
plined training sessions before they took to the streets and lunch-
counters. It was not engrained in their congenital nature; they
proved to themselves and their enemies that it worked. Non-
violent behavior sometimes impressed the opponent; it always
altered the character of the practitioner. These few learned about
poverty firsthand: that while it drains the energies of a people,
there is a dignity that remains and an unbelievable sharing of
limited resources. Especially from the black mothers in the homes
where these whites found themselves they witnessed a profound
level of communal living. The sacrifices forced upon these few
whites could hardly compare to the generations of sustenance-
living imposed upon the blacks they came to know intimately.

Surely none of these whites regret the choice they made, nor
would they likely refuse to repeat their stand if they had their lives
to live over. Sure, it was tough, it was scary, it was dangerous, and
life-threatening. On the other hand, it brought them a reward that
money cannot buy. It brought them a new experience, a spiritual
renewal from walking alongside a people being led by God from
the wilderness of oppression into a land of freedom. No matter
what the hardships they endured they could say at their life's end,
"We were there!"

THESE FEW ALSO PAID A PRICE

INTRODUCTION

While Martin Luther King Jr. in his "Letter from Birmingham Jail" (1963) bemoaned the fact that the religious leaders of the white South failed to support his civil rights crusade, he nonetheless confessed that a few "have marched with us down nameless streets of the South. They have languished in filthy, roach-infested jails, suffering the abuse and brutality of angry policemen who see them as 'dirty nigger lovers.'" In this book, I have spotlighted some of these white Southerners. They did not see themselves as heroes or heroines; they simply took a stand along-side their black brothers and sisters to correct a cultural wrong (Jim Crowism), to stand up for American democracy, and, in most cases, to affirm their faith in a God of universal human brother-hood. For that stand, they faced the brutality of most of their com-patriots, a degree of brutality and rejection that is now hard to believe. As one of them put it, they were subjected to the "four B's"—bullets, beatings, bombings, and burnings. Yet, the physical abuse was perhaps not as severe as the psychological and social alienation, so powerfully administered that in a few cases the victims were forced to remove themselves from their homeland.

It was not easy to uncover the names and histories of "these few whites who also paid a price." The reason is quite clear: during the time of their witness, the last thing they wanted was publicity, to have the glare of the media focused upon themselves. That would merely invite a cross burning in front of their domicile, a shot-in-the-night from a hidden assailant, an endless stream of retaliatory insults and slights as they went about their daily lives. The second reason pertains to the nature of the Southern media. With few exceptions, the Southern newspaper editors were not likely to feature their actions in a positive manner, nor to write encouraging editorials in their behalf. For instance, even the praised liberal editor of the *Atlanta Journal*, Ralph McGill, could hardly stomach the native Georgian, Lillian Smith, who wrote countless books and articles supporting King and the Civil Rights Movement. Thus, the persons cited in this book enjoyed a virtual blackout in the pages of the news media. When they were mentioned, it was most likely in a negative posture.

Fortunately, some of the persons cited in this book decided to set the record straight by writing their own memoirs of the crucial events in which they were key participants. After more than a generation, a goodly number of these memoirs are available to us. Others, however, felt the pain and the shame they had endured to be more than they could face a second time: they wanted to forget it. One even committed suicide. To bring their personal stories to light, the author had to do a lot of probing over the past forty years, pressing family members and friends to release what details they privately possessed. Naturally, in the process of this research, many more deserving witnesses must have fallen through the cracks.

What appears in this book, then, is an attempt to present a representative profile of certain Southerners (two or three who adopted the South as their homeland) whom King pin-pointed in his Birmingham Letter. They represent a cross-section of the general population: some key public officials, some housewives; some clergy, some laity; some highly educated, some ordinary citizens; some men, some women; and, what is probably most noteworthy, these representatives were scattered throughout the South rather than in one or two concentrated centers of cultural criticism. Fact is, they come from eleven different states from Texas to West Virginia. Their personal witnesses present another viewpoint to the traditional "Solid South," white, that is. What is more remarkable is that in these individuals we possess a counterbalance to "man's inhumanity to man." The stories told in this book do not make a pretty picture. But they must be told so that our nation—or any other nation on earth—may not repeat such inhumanity.

Finally, let it be clear that none of the principals in this book claim that their trials and sufferings were greater than their fellowblacks engaged in the Civil Rights Movement. Nor would the author of this collection dare make such a false comparison. Almost any black person reared under the Jim Crow system with its arbitrary discrimination, its harsh strictures, and the customary cruel enforcement of its White Racism Code would have suffered more. And it goes without saying that the thousands of blacks who dared challenge the unjust laws—those who were jailed, beaten, hosed down, bitten by dogs, and some times murdered—took the brunt of white resistance to change. If there was any difference in the treatment of blacks and whites, it was in the vehemence with which many whites accosted the few whites involved in civil rights. For these Southern whites, those civil rights workers were "traitors" to the Southern way of life. They had sided with "the enemy" and must be whipped back into line. They had violated the sacred code of white supremacy and must be punished. Throughout the South, these attitudes prevailed, for the most part, from the highest legal levels to the street gangs (sometimes including moms) yelling curses at them as they marched with blacks. The modest accomplishment of this book may be to clothe in flesh-and-blood the anonymous whites whom King recognized as colleagues in the civil rights struggle. And to see that they also paid a price.

ED KING

The white preacher was addressing the mostly black mourners at the funeral service for James Chaney on 7 August 1964 at the First Union Baptist Church in Meridian, Mississippi. (Chaney was the black killed and buried in a Neshoba County farm pond dam along with the other two white civil rights workers, Michael Schwermer and Andrew Goodman.) "I come before you now; some of you know me, some of you don't. I'm a Mississippian. I'm the chaplain at Tougaloo College. I ran for lieutenant governor with Aaron Henry last fall; my wife is from Jackson, Mississippi. My parents used to live in Vicksburg before they were run out of Mississippi. By the same kind of people who do this kind of thing and the silent people who, I think, are just as guilty and more damned in their souls because they know it's wrong. I come before you to try to say that my brothers have killed my brothers. My white brothers have killed my black brothers. But here in Mississippi people like Ed King from Vicksburg and James Chaney from Meridian are not supposed to know each other as brothers..."[1]

The minister was Ed King, who had graduated from Millsaps College in Jackson, Mississippi, in 1958, and who, while pursuing theological graduate training, had assisted in the 1960 sit-in

---

[1] Biographical notes given the author by Ed King in several communications and personal interview, Fall 1999.

campaign in the Montgomery Movement started by Martin Luther King Jr., and had returned to Jackson in 1963 to become chaplain at a black college. Meanwhile, he was ordained by the white Methodist Conference of Mississippi in 1961, but stripped of the possibility of any clerical appointment in 1963 by a vote of 89 to 85. His thoroughgoing dedication to the state's Civil Rights Movement had "labeled" him. But, far more notorious was his record of arrests while engaged daily in the Movement.

In March 1960, he commenced his civil rights activities by acting as an intermediary between the jailed Montgomery protesters and the local white ministers and church women. He had not intended to be arrested, but on March 31, he found himself in the black-owned Regal Cafe at lunch with an interracial group of activists. Twenty persons in all were arrested and charged with disorderly conduct—behavior "calculated to create a breach of the peace," as the Judge phrased it. On 7 June, two hours after receiving a $100 fine for the earlier arrest, he was arrested a second time for lunching with a black friend in the Jefferson Davis Hotel where he was residing. He was convicted of trespassing in his own hotel and sentenced to hard labor for a week. He became abruptly aware that this was no Sunday school picnic. He phrased his predicament to a reporter in religious terms: "I consider myself in approximately the same situation as early Christians who were put to death for refusing to put incense on the statue of the emperor. We refused to put a pinch of incense on the idol of segregation."[2] Any hope of an ordinary Methodist parish appointment vanished, and his parents back in Mississippi were hounded out of the state. Through his friendship with Medgar Evers (soon to be assassinated by White Citizens Council thugs), he won the Tougaloo chaplaincy. From that base, for the next six years, he would be at the center of the Mississippi campaign. His first year there he was

---

[2] Ibid.

arrested five times on alleged traffic violations; three of those times he was thrown in jail. Also, that first year he led the campaign to integrate the leading white churches of Jackson. During the Mississippi Freedom Summer of 1964, he was virtual chaplain of the hundreds of student workers who entered the state. The same year he helped found the Mississippi Freedom Democratic Party, served as a delegate to the Democratic National Conventions of 1964, '68, and '72, and ran for Congress on the MFDP ticket in 1966. During those days, he was often jailed, beaten, and sometimes hospitalized. Being the child of the church, reared by Christian parents, trained in a Methodist college, he finally admitted: "But the church had not prepared me for the level of white resistance in Mississippi or the rest of the South."[3]

He pin-points that white cruelty in describing his jail experience in Montgomery, July 1960: "In the white unit the other prisoners were told by the guards who brought me in that I was a 'nigger loving agitator' involved in the sit-in demonstrations. The guard gave the toughest looking of the white prisoners a newspaper with a photograph of a black coed leader and me together. The white prisoner beat me several times and I tried to protest to the white guards but no one would come to the cell door where I was shouting for help. The white prisoner just laughed and cursed me. He pushed others on into slugging me more. He laughed and said he knew the guards would not return till morning and would not help me. He made lots of talk about interracial sex and that he would make me 'eat' the black woman in the photograph. He then beat me until I began eating the newspaper. I choked and gagged and he finally let me tear the paper into strips which I could swallow eventually, between fist blows to my head. At one point I started to spit, almost to vomit, and he knocked me to the floor and stomped my head into the

---

[3] Ibid.

concrete, chipping several front teeth. Then my tormentor announced to all in the room that I would be killed during the night....Later my attorney informed me that the brutality was to discourage me from appealing my case to the Federal Courts and assured me that the white judge, prosecutor, and all the police involved knew in advance that I was to be beaten by a cell-mate."[4]

Ed King was now a marked man, having accomplished the ultimate in the betrayal of his Southern white culture. He was not merely assisting the local Blacks in their protests for equal rights; he was employed by them, residing with his family in an integrated compound, and making the media headlines almost every day as the most visible white Mississippi native to publicly defend the Freedom Movement. Police kept a daily watch on his movements; police escorts followed him to town on his every family errand; at night, unmarked cars forced him off the road, once wrecking his car in an accident that left him maimed; a bomb exploded near his home; and most ironic of all, the voter registrar would not qualify him to vote in the very election where he was on the ballot as a third party candidate for lieutenant governor.

Following the funeral for slain Medgar Evers, the state civil rights leader on 12 June 1963, over 5,000 mourners who had walked behind the casket were charged by the police. Ed King was seized in the mass arrest of demonstrators and was singled out for unusual mistreatment and torture. As the police van entered the gate of the now feared Fairgrounds Prison, an officer peered in and asked if King was among them. He then instructed the guard, "Close the doors, and let them sweat awhile." All King could think of was that this sweatbox was so like the Nazi railway cars crammed with victims. King has written an account of what happened next:

---
[4] Ibid.

"We joined a line of prisoners forced to lean, face forward, against a wall with our hands outstretched above our heads, braced against the wall. Whenever any one of us would groan or cry and begin to drop our arms or shift the position of our bodies, the guards would walk up, curse us, and sometimes poke us with their guns or clubs. 'Hey, you bastard, what do you think this is? Straighten out your damn arms. Reach higher, higher on that wall!' Although I wanted to scream and drop to the ground, to twist and curl my body to relieve the agony and pain of the position, I would respond to the order. Since I was already bruised from being dragged when captured, I felt the intended pain of this 'magnolia torture' quickly. There was absolutely no reason for being forced to stand like this.

"The man standing next to me had been badly beaten. On the back of his head was an ugly patch of blood. Flecks of bright, fresh blood oozed out of the wound. I found what little courage I still had and slowly turned my head in his direction. When I saw flies crawling on the wound, I was sick. I no longer cared about the guards. I dropped my arms, pulled a handkerchief from my pocket and moved toward the wounded man. An officer shouted, 'Hey, King, what the hell are you doing out of line?' Before I had a chance of reasoning with him, he raised his rifle in the air, 'You nigger-loving son of a bitch. What the hell you think this is, a damn hospital? I know you ain't no damn doctor. Shit, you ain't no preacher either. You touch his head, and you get one just like it.' Slowly, I turned away from the injured man. I would not bind up his wounds. I turned away from the sweat and the filth, from the flies and the blood. I saw only the danger to myself, I heard only the threat to me. There was no courage, no goodness, no decency left, only fear. I managed to speak to the guard, 'I understand you, sir; I know what you can do.' I looked at the guards and I knew that if they did this work day after day they could invent torture worthy of the Nazis. I knew these ordinary folk could administer death camps and ovens as easily as any Nazis. I thought that if I was ever in an American death camp I might be so afraid, so broken down in spirit, that I might be a docile prisoner tool of the guards. I had always wondered why the prisoners of the Germans did not organize themselves and revolt. Now I know. Any of us could be good Mississippians, good Germans. Those were the thoughts I had part of the time I stood in line. But mostly my thoughts centered on my pain."[5]

The year 1964 marked the peak of the "Mississippi Burnings"—a euphemism for the fact that once every week for over a year some Black church was fired. Churches were targeted since they were the centers of voter-registration. King and all the other civil rights workers lived in constant fear for their lives. Many have reported since, "We all expected to die that summer." King's account follows: "Fear was always with us, a constant, abiding Presence: fear of pain and violence (certain in jail, possible anywhere, anytime); fear of the sudden whim of any white policeman—and his guns, his clubs, his dogs; fear of thirst, hunger, and isolation in prison; fear of the forces of evil revealed in the hate stares of so many white men and women and children; fear of the night for the danger that could come skulking in the deep darkness that followed the beauty of the setting sun, of the long post-midnight hours when Mississippi slittered to destroy its enemies; fear of the day, of the rising of the sun when the first heat of the morning meant you had to go out from the shelter and attack Mississippi; fear of the stifling heat of a freedom house in late summer; fear of the power of hate and of the weakness of love. Fear that had frozen the hearts of the church-goers and

---

[5] Thomas R. West and James W. Moon, ed., *To Redeem a Nation, A History and Anthology of the Civil Rights Movement* (St. James, N.Y.:Brandywine Press, 1993) 137.

immobilized the white moderates; the paranoid fear of change and of outsiders; the fear of brotherhood/sisterhood. Fear, and the very fear of fear, built the Terror in the souls of all of us in the Mississippi Movement."[6]

In spite of his valiant, courageous and continuous leadership in the Deep South's Freedom Movement—still insisting that he could persuade the moderates, appeal to the Christian sentiments of the church-going populace, and bring Mississippi to its senses, holding firmly to his non-violent stance—King came to the conclusion he was residing in a police-state. Nothing revealed this fact more than the 1963 day white police crashed into the Tougaloo College chapel. The worship service was under way that October morning; the police were well aware of where King was located at any other hour during the seven-day week, twenty-four hours a day. Yet, two brown-shirted deputy sheriffs pushed aside the ushers, banged open the sanctuary inner doors, and noisily tramped down the aisle toward the altar. "The church was silent except for my voice so the heavy steps of the police rushing down the aisle were heard by every one of the several hundred students and faculty gathered for prayers. One of them moved toward the pulpit waving his paper and ignoring my praying and loudly saying, 'Hey, King, take this summons!' I ended the prayer as the policeman cast his document down on the open pulpit Bible. The paper slid off the Bible and down to the floor. The congregation was shocked and now began the buzz of angered whispers. I nodded to the organist and announced a hymn. The choir began to sing, the congregation stood and joined the hymn of faith as the storm troopers walked back the central aisle. The officers left off the final touch—all they needed to do was click their heels, extend their arms, and shout 'Seig, Heil!'"[7]

---

[6] Biographical notes given the author by Ed King.
[7] West and Moon, *To Redeem a Nation*, 142.

Anne Moody, author of the popular book, *Coming of Age in Mississippi*, was a student in Tougaloo College at the time of this police intrusion. She was deeply involved in the civil rights protests and was repeatedly jailed. When Ed King commenced his chaplaincy at the college, Anne shared the opinion of most students: here was just another white paternalistic guy temporarily "slumming" in the black ghetto. But once they had shed blood together in the protests, once she watched his courage under fire, once she rode over-night to the Washington March with Ed and Mrs. King, and once she became almost their adopted daughter, she changed her mind. In her account of her graduation exercises, which not a single member of her family attended because of their objection to her engagement in the protests, she tells of becoming so sick that afterwards she found refuge in the King home. "Mrs. King gave me a hot cup of tea and a couple of aspirins. Then Reverend King carried us to Steven's Kitchenette and ordered five of the biggest steaks in the house. As we were all sitting there eating, I looked at Reverend King. And silently, I asked him to forgive—forgive me for doubting him when he first came to Tougaloo. I think because he was a white native Mississippian almost every student doubted him at that time. We had never before had a white Southerner on our faculty. I used to look at Mrs. King going in and out of the chapel after visiting Reverend King and just hated the thought of a white Southern minister and his wife taking over the most beautiful and cherished building on the campus. Now sitting across the table from them I realized I had more respect for them than any white person I had ever known."[8]

---

[8] Ann Moody, *Coming of Age in Mississippi* (N.Y.: Dial Pre ss, 1962) 343.

JOAN TRUMPAUER

In 1960, Joan Trumpauer, a twenty-year old just finishing her freshman year at Duke University, made a major decision: she decided to transfer to Tougaloo College in Jackson, Mississippi. Her family and most of her friends thought it a foolish move; in their minds she was transferring from the top school of the South to the most backward. Tougaloo was a Black institution, and Joan was daring to become the first white student enrolled there in the twentieth century. She was a Southerner, from Annandale, Virginia, with a long line of loyal Southerners on her mother's side from Georgia, where she spent many holidays. She had been reared in the bosom of white supremacy culture.

That decision turned her life up side down. Within the next two years, she was jailed five times for demonstrating against racial segregation in six states. She served a two-month prison-term in the notorious Parchman Penitentiary in Mississippi, and her life was threatened by white supremist thugs on several occasions. All the while, she maintained an A-scholastic record at Tougaloo and mostly earned her own college expenses beyond a scholarship she won. From June 1961 to May 1964, when she graduated, Joan was the center of many Tugaloo generated civil rights protests. So much so, that Anne Moody, her closest friend on campus and later noted for her celebrated book, *Coming of Age in Mississippi*, unconsciously repeats the phrase "Joan and I." In fact, Joan had "recruited" Anne. "During the summer," Anne wrote in her book, "a white student moved into the room across the hall from me. Her name was Joan Trumpauer, and she told me she worked for SNCC. In a short time, we got to know each other very well, and soon I was going into Jackson with Joan and hanging out at her office. SNCC was starting a voter registration drive in the Delta and was recruiting students from Tougaloo. When they asked me if I wanted to canvass every other weekend, I agreed to go."[1]

Together they were such a team that they made the Klan blacklist. The KKK circulated posters with photographs of the persons they targeted to kill. Joan's, Anne's, and Ed King's (Tougaloo's white chaplain) were prominently displayed. X's were marked across the faces of those they had already killed, such as Medgar Evers. It was a scary time to be working for democracy in America. Joan and Anne were partners in the infamous Woolworth's sit-in of 1963 in Jackson. Anne's book reports what occurred: "At noon, students from a nearby white high school started pouring in to Woolworth's. When they first saw us they were sort of surprised. They didn't know how to react. A few started to heckle. Then the white students started chanting all kinds of anti-Negro slogans. We were called a little bit of everything. A couple of boys took one end of a nearby rope and made it into a hangman's noose. Several attempts were made to put it around our necks....We kept our eyes straight forward and did not look at the crowd....Memphis (a fellow-student) suggested that we pray. We bowed our heads and all hell broke loose. A man reached forward, threw Memphis from his seat, and slapped my face. Then another man who worked in the store threw me against an adjoining counter. Down on my knees on the floor, I saw Memphis lying near the lunch counter with blood running out of

---

[1] Anne Moody, *Coming of Age in Mississippi* (N.Y.: Dial Press, 1968) 224.

the corners of his mouth."[2] In the *Newsweek* magazine photograph of this Woolworth fiasco, dated July 29, 1963, Joan and Anne are pictured side by side in the bloody mess.

Joan had had some harsh preparation for this encounter. Working for SNCC in Washington, D.C. in 1961, she had helped organize the Freedom Rides. She herself later rode with Stokeley Carmichael on the train from New Orleans to Jackson where they were subsequently arrested upon arriving at the Jackson railway station. She was sentenced to two months imprisonment and $200 fine. Conditions in the Parchman Prison were as bad as its reputation, but Joan managed to endure the cruelty by playing solitaire with cards she fashioned from scrap paper, by reading Gandhian philosophy, keeping a diary sewed in her skirt hem, and writing cheerful letters to her parents who offered to pay for her release although not in sympathy with her crusade. Writing to her little sister on her birthday, she quipped,

"Roses are red, violets are blue;
  I'm still at Parchman, Happy birthday to you."

During what was dubbed "Freedom Summer 1964"—in the state of Mississippi, a car driven by Reverend Ed King, with Mrs. Jeanette King, Joan Trumpauer, and a Tougaloo sociology professor as passengers, was attacked about midnight on Highway #55 near Canton. A caravan of Ku Klux Klanners approached suddenly from the rear. One car swung around in front, forcing King's car to stop. About fifteen white men immediately surrounded the car. They had clubs, guns, and one large gasoline can. When they were about to break the windows, the professor rolled his window halfway down to try and reason with them. He was hit on the side of the head and blood came spurting out. They

[2] Ibid., 236.

hesitated a moment, talking among themselves. Then they let the King car leave after everyone inside had promised never to return to Canton. Joan Trumpauer later reported, "If I have ever been close to death it was that night."[3] Joan's determination and social conscience dates back to the U.S. Supreme Court desegregation of the schools decision of 1954. Although only thirteen at the time, she was acutely aware of the school crisis, especially within the state of Virginia where politicians were planning massive resistance. As a teenager, she organized discussion groups within her Presbyterian church to prepare students for her school's impending integration. Her early Christian ideals were in sharp conflict with the South she loved. Later on, in the midst of the Civil Rights Movement, when asked why she was willing to brave so much punishment, she promptly replied, "I'm trying to help America become what it says it is, as a Southerner I'm trying to improve, not destroy our way of life; I'm a Christian who has read the Declaration of Independence."[4]

---

[3] Ibid., 341.
[4] Alex Poinsett, "Integration in Mississippi," article on Joan Trumpauer, *Ebony Magazine* (January 1963): 28.

PAT CUSICK

Pat Cusick was a native Alabamian, an Air Force volunteer in the Korean War, a worker supporting his mother when he returned to America to live in Rome, Georgia. He later quit his job to enroll in Belmont Abbey College in North Carolina, and by 1963 had graduated from the University of North Carolina. He was a large man, at age thirty-two weighing about two hundred pounds. Now in May 1963, he found himself being arrested, hauled to the police station in Chapel Hill, and being brutally man-handled. As he tells it, "Officers began kicking him, even as they carried him inside the building. He looked up and saw that they were about to ram his head into a steel post at the corner of the stairway. 'I struggled to try to keep my head out of the way, and supposedly when I did that, I kicked one of the policeman. They put me down on the floor, sat on my back and started kicking my ribs, and they put the wrist clamps on my wrists and started bending my wrists....And it was almost ironical, because then Chief Blake came on the scene, and they stopped and they took me down to the cell, and one came down about a half-hour later and read out a warrant on me for assaulting a policeman with a deadly weapon, the weapon being my shoe, and I had to listen to that. Then they took me over to the hospital and X-rayed me.'"[1] This was the experience of the person

---

[1] John Ehle, *The Free Men* (N. Y.: Harper and Row, 1965) 178.

who first organized the Chapel Hill freedom protests of 1963 and '64, and who, as he admitted later, was so inexperienced at non-violent protesting, that "the first time I ever picketed I felt foolish," and who for days on end taught the thousands of local protesters—consisting of blacks and whites, high school students, college students, municipal adults and some university faculty—the Gandhian tactics of nonviolence. In all, over the two-year period over 1,500 were arrested.

Chapel Hill, North Carolina, where the most liberal university of the South was located and where its liberalism was supposed to have over-flowed among its townspeople, was the last place expected to experience such massive demonstrations and such severe legal punishment imposed upon those arrested. "Why us?" its citizens asked defensively. "Don't we have an excellent record in race matters? The university had admitted its first Negro graduate student in 1951. The public schools were partially integrated. One member of the school board was black, elected in 1958, and one alderman, elected in 1953, was black. Two of its policemen were black, and altogether the city, the university, and the hospital hired about a thousand black workers. So why Chapel Hill?" Above-and-beyond these minimal facts was the attitude of the prevailing liberalism: "We are making such progress that we do not need these street demonstrations. In fact, these tactics of direct action will only arouse latent opposition and spoil the good will which prevails." Dean Brandis of the University Law School spoke for these liberals: "It is not more saintly to engage in criminal activity because one disapproves the law being violated than, as in the case of the traffic-blocking, to engage in such activity because one disapproves of some other law or some general condition in the community. At least, if this is saintly, then Barnett, Wallace, and General Walker are equally entitled to canonization....There is no possibility that more complete equal justice can be achieved for the Negro through the destruction of public order."[2]

Pat Cusick and the few other conscientious persons feeling the need to prod the community and who accordingly formed the Committee for Open Business in early May, 1963, saw things differently. So did the student newspaper, the *Daily Tar Heel*. In an editorial, it responded to Dean Brandis: "We believe (non-violent civil disobedience) is justified under certain circumstances and when done in a non-violent, submissive manner—which, Dean Brandis, is the difference between Martin Luther King and Gov. George Wallace. Then civil disobedience is not only justified but desirable in that it serves as a safety valve for frustration and prevents frustration from deteriorating into despair..."[3] The paper did its own survey of the town's so-called progress. It reported that the three white motels did not accept Negro lodgers. Thirty-two percent of the local restaurants maintain segregation. Of the nine establishments serving beer and ale, five do not have equal service. What Cusick's group, COB, shockingly discovered was that opposition to their campaign originated not with the Klan, or the common citizenry, but from the very liberalism for which the town was so famous—a situation so markedly different from the sources of the massive resistance throughout the remainder of the South.

In a letter Pat wrote to a friend on 2 August 1963, he explained his amazement: "When we staged this first sit-in, the town's lid flew off literally and completely. Each time we do something new, the cry of alarm goes up and we are denounced, in a large part by people who tell us, 'We believe in your goal, but not your method.' After we staged our sit-in, the *Chapel Hill Weekly* in a front-page editorial said the leaders of the COB had 'a lust for power, for revenge, or a neurotic need for martyrdom.' The executive

---

[2] Ibid., 204.
[3] Ibid., 243.

committee of the COB tried to figure out who among us had the lust for power and against whom we had the desire for revenge."[4] In any case, the Board of Alderman corroborated the degree of municipal resistance to getting rid of segregation by voting not to pass a city ordinance prohibiting discrimination in its businesses. The COB members now disheartened by their failure to influence the Aldermen reorganized themselves into a much stronger and much larger Freedom Committee. The protests and subsequent arrests now increased drastically.

However, it was in the courts and the prison system that the protesters encountered their major prejudice. And Pat Cusick became the primary victim. When the Superior Court convened in Hillsboro at the Christmas season in 1964, it was presided over by the most conservative Judge Raymond Mallard. Speaking later to a church group, he pontificated: "I have tried people who teach others and who in the name of Christ are advocating the breaking of the laws of the land...Of all this disturbance that we have seen in the name of religion....the greater portion of it is a prostitution of religion, and we are being duped by that kind of people."[5] Not surprisingly, then, were the severe penalties he imposed when sentencing the convicted civil rights protesters. When Cusick's turn came, Judge Mallard asked him if he had anything further to say. Having nothing to add, Cusick stood expecting a sentence of no more than six months. The Judge said that there were two counts against him, and he had decided to sentence him to serve one year of hard labor on the state roads; on the second count, to two years of hard labor on the state roads. Then he relented by suspending the second sentence and placing Cusick on a five-year probation, during which time he was "not to engage in or be a part of, or physically accompany any person or persons engaged in any

---

[4] Ibid., 88.
[5] Ibid., 244.

demonstrations for any cause, on any public street, highway or sidewalk, or any other public place in North Carolina."[6] Judge Mallard had apparently decided Pat Cusick was the ring leader of the whole series of protests and that he would thoroughly muzzle him. Professor Dan Pollitt of the University Law School observed that he had not found any sentencing in American jurisprudence to equal the severity of Judge Mallard's decrees.

After a night in the Hillsboro jail, Pat Cusick was taken to the road camp in Durham County. On arrival, Pat told the prison captain that he wanted to be transferred to an integrated camp, if there was one, or to a Negro camp. He said he believed segregation was wrong both inside and outside prisons, and he announced that unless this was done he would refuse to eat or work. The guards were less than impressed by this unexpected request; so when they took him to the cellblock with seventy-five other prisoners, they bellowed: "Here's one of those nigger-loving sons of bitches. He says he's not going to eat or work, because he'd rather be with niggers than with you guys." Soon a fellow prisoner informed Pat that the guards had been encouraging the prisoners to molest this "new fellow." "He told me I would probably get killed during the night and advised me not to go to sleep." [7]After two days of fasting, the major of the North Carolina Prison Department interviewed Pat and concluded he should be put into solitary confinement for the remainder of his prison term. There, in a bare cell, he lay for days, with headaches pounding him night and day. As he put it later: "He contemplated the remarkable example of himself, a single being in revolt against the world, an Alabamian starving because of an issue that would have been repulsive to his ancestors and that would have been repulsive to him when a child....Yet by the God he no longer quite understood or formally accepted, he

---

[6] Ibid., 274.
[7] Ibid., 119.

would not eat."[8] Then word reached him that he was to be transferred to the State Penitentiary for medical observation. As he stumbled toward the gate, he asked one of his fellow prisoners, "How many days have I been here?" "Six," the man replied.

Cusick was subsequently transferred to the Sandy Ridge Prison between Greensboro and Winston-Salem, where he was due to complete his sentence. Each cellblock slept eight to ten prisoners, with a long row of cots, toilets, and a wood or coal stove at each end of the room. Here, also, his fellow prisoners were in disbelief that he could be "sent up" for a year just for "helping get them niggers off the street." "No, no," Pat tried to explain, "I was helping the Negroes who were on the street protesting for their rights." That was beyond their comprehension. His fellow prisoners were merely echoing the state's top politicians. At the moment, United States Senator Sam Ervin was opposing President Johnson's Civil Rights Bill: "The pending civil rights proposals are the most monstrous blueprint for government tyranny presented to an American Congress since George Washington took the oath of office."[9] At the same time, the gubernatorial candidates were vying with each other as to who was the most racist, with Supreme Court Justice, I. Beverly Lake, taking the lead in that regard.

On the other hand, there were a few Chapel Hillians who came to Pat and the other imprisoned civil rights protesters' aid. John Ehle worked hard to get them paroled. He secured a job offer and a place of residence for Pat and convinced the Parole Board to release him. In August 1964, Pat was released and immediately flew to John Ehle's apartment in New York City. "He arrived at my apartment, stunned by the shock of prison and the even greater shock of suddenly being out of prison."[10] Frank Porter Graham,

---

[8] Ibid., 121.
[9] Ibid., 203.
[10] Ibid., 310.

the world-renown liberal past-president of the university felt the protest movement no more than "part of the unfolding American Revolution in its modern phase." Ehle concludes, "I suspect it was this new youth movement which struck Chapel Hill. It was not a lightning bolt from alien lands; it was native American, actually native Southern, and whether we like it or not it is ours."[11]

---

[11] Ibid., 331.

MARY KING

Mary King's family connections with southwestern Virginia and Surry, the border-county in North Carolina, reach back five generations. Her great-great-great-grandfather was a Methodist preacher from Surry and her own father was a Methodist preacher residing in Spotsylvania County of Virginia at the time of her civil rights activity in Danville, Virginia. With this background, it is understandable that there would be considerable consternation among her kinspeople about her involvement with the Student Nonviolent Coordinating Committee. As late as 1976, a hate-message produced by the White Citizen Council of Shreveport, Louisiana, targeted her broadcasting on the main radio station of Surry County: "The most powerful woman in the Jimmy Carter apparatus is the same white woman who ran with a pack of Negro criminals during the 1960s." It blamed Stokely Carmichael and Mary King, "a grinning wide-eyed white woman" with a "fierce glare," for the "ruin, riot, rape, and revolution in the Deep South."[1]

Yet, her engrained sense of justice was derived from the very same Southern milieu. She credits her father's own conscientious sensibilities for "the eventful Easter week of 1962 when I met John Lewis, Bernard Lafayette, Jim Forman, and Julian Bond (and)

---

[1] Mary King, *Freedom Song* (N.Y.: William Morrow Publishers, 1987) 115.

concluded that I should go to work for SNNC...In a sense, I was shaped for that decision from the time I could talk. As I was growing up, my father would not let me forget that, as a youth in Virginia, he was shielded from any historical references that might reflect on the prevailing segregated patterns around him. To my father, a scholar, this omission was proof that racism and segregation affected Southern whites as it did blacks, denying both groups full humanity. If, he reasoned, in the interests of justifying segregation, the basics of American history had been denied and distorted in one of the South's best universities (Washington and Lee which he attended), then all Southerners were the losers. 'I would rather be robbed than to rob, and I would rather have been enslaved than to have enslaved,' he would tell me, believing it more destructive to the human spirit to be the oppressor than the oppressed."[2]

On 21 December 1963, Mary King, at the age of 23, was an office employee in the Atlanta headquarters of SNCC. She had chosen to rent an apartment in the black section of the city, and was thoroughly enjoying the challenge of her civil rights work. That night a Kenya diplomat had addressed a SNCC gathering at a downtown hotel. Afterwards, when several of the SNCC workers decided to get a cup of coffee at the Toddle House restaurant next door, they were refused service, and police were called. "Two paddy wagons pulled up and several police officers entered the restaurant and began arresting us. Without consultation with each other, but because of previous training and preparation, each of us went limp as we were arrested, making no resistance but refusing to cooperate by walking to the paddy wagon....Twenty-one of us were hauled off to the Atlanta city jail, nicknamed Big Rock, downtown near the gold-domed capitol building of the state of Georgia...'Here's some damned white girls who say they're colored,' one of the officers processing us called out jeeringly to his supervisor in

---

[2] Ibid., 53.

another room. 'Whatcha want us to do with 'em?' They looked at us with hostility and scorn and charged us with violation of the state's anti-trespassing law."[3] In those days, SNCC's policy was "Jail—no bail." So Mary spent the next five days quivering in jail, as much afraid of her cellmates as of the guards. Her uncle died unexpectedly, and the SNCC officials felt she should be released to attend his funeral in Virginia. Back home, after her hurried flight from Atlanta, she now had to worry how her large extended family would receive her—as several kins-persons had previously express-ed their displeasure at her involvement with SNCC. In a dramatic moment, as she entered the room for the first time to greet every-one, her mother rushed up to embrace her, exclaiming, "So, there's my little jailbird!"

Mary King felt that SNCC was her larger family. "Running through the organization, like a low-voltage current, was a sense that being part of the SNCC staff set you apart from everyone else. I certainly felt it. I don't think there was anyone who didn't believe that he or she was part of a singular American phenomenon....It was a conviction that no one could match us; and indeed within the overall Civil Rights Movement, no one could equal our pas-sionate belief in democracy, our concept of indigenous leadership, our unwillingness to bow to authority...Despite the passage of more than twenty years, I still feel I was part of something so extraordinary that it almost defies description. I did not picture myself a fugitive, nor did I any longer have the sensation of being under siege as I had in Danville. I felt that we were inimitable. I was sure that we were closer to the truth than anyone else."[4]

Her reference to "the siege mentality" pertains to her own harrowing experience in the protests of Danville, Virginia in 1963. During several weeks of SNCC-led demonstrations, over six

---

[3] Ibid., 175.
[4] Ibid., 439.

hundred were arrested and jailed, and their mistreatment was as bad as that experienced in the Birmingham protests of 1963. The Corporation Court grand jury had found and dusted off an archaic Virginia statute that held that it was illegal "to incite the colored population to acts of violence and war against the white population." When the grand jury held its hearing leading to the 21 June (1963) indictments, no one subpoenaed was allowed to bring an attorney. Len Holt, their lawyer, was himself served an indictment and had to spend three days in jail. Holt came to Mary in the middle of the night with apparent urgency. He anticipated that Mary would be indicted under this statute, and he advised her to escape at once. She demurred; but he insisted. While she lay hidden on the floorboard of the vehicle, she was taken across the state line into North Carolina and housed in a Catholic nunnery. That day the grand jury handed down her indictment for "inciting acts of violence and war." That was the welcome she received from the town where her father had attended junior college and where her Methodist great-great-great grandfather had spent the night when he walked the 275 miles to Richmond to be ordained.

That her civil rights participation gave more to Mary King than she contributed to it is her own estimate. "The Civil Rights Movement gave me the ideal testing ground with all its exhaustion, strain, and tension. The demands were inordinate and there was very little in the way of extended release. Just because I was white, I could not slip away from the black community into the white community and achieve another state of mind like shedding a jacket—not that I ever wanted to. I carried with me everywhere, even in solitude, a sense of myself as working for the movement. The struggle gave me the chance to learn to push past my emotional limits—if I did my job just a little better or worked a little longer, I might save someone's life or avert a tragedy."[5]

[5] Ibid., 211.

JONATHAN DANIELS

Some people say that the tough military regimen at Virginia Military Institute where Jonathan Daniels spent four years prepared him to brave the abuse heaped upon him by the white people of Lowndes County, Alabama, during the summer of 1965. Others claim the religious epiphany he had experienced pertaining to the "Magnificat" found in the daily prayers of his Episcopal Church—"He has put down the mighty from their thrones, and exalted them of low degree; He has filled the hungry with good things, and the rich he has sent empty away"—fortified Jonathan with rare mystical powers. In either case, living as a white among blacks in Lowndes County (the poorest county in the state and with the reputation of severe white oppression of its black majority population—as late as 1965, not one of the nearly 6,000 eligible blacks was registered to vote) demanded superhuman courage. Because of its notorious race relations over the decades, it was known as "Bloody Lowndes." Located between Selma and Montgomery, even the most seasoned civil rights workers tried to avoid the county. Jonathan Daniels, known throughout his boyhood and even at VMI as a gentle and delicate youth, now found himself placed where the strongest and toughest white civil rights workers would not venture, as a volunteer with the Student

Nonviolent Coordinating Committee's summer campaign to register black voters in the county.

This summer campaign (1965) was his second engagement in Alabama. Earlier that year, during the spring months, he had been living in Selma working under the auspices of the Episcopal Society for Cultural and Religious Unity, specifically assigned to assist SNCC. New to the Deep South, he found his role both baffling and dangerous. The blatant racial injustice and white hostility to his presence left him bewildered and angry. His innocence and immaturity had left him totally unprepared for what he encountered in Selma. He reluctantly admitted "(I) would like to get a high-powered rifle and take to the woods (to) fight the battle as the klans-men do...This is grim business—it might as well be war."[6] His outer psyche was still wearing the uniform of his intense military training, but his inner soul was deeply troubled. On April 6, he traveled with a group of civil rights workers who went to aid a demonstration in the nearby town of Camden. The next day, on the eighth day of attempted marches by the demonstrators, the police threw tear gas canisters into their midst. Daniels recklessly picked up one that rolled near his feet and hurled it away. Instantly the police took Daniels and another white into custody, but they were released in a few minutes, probably out of respect for their clerical collars. That experience changed his attitude toward the tactics of non-violence: his commitment had been tested and strengthened. He wrote afterwards: "My hostility lasted really until last week. I think it was when I got tear-gassed in Camden that I began to change. I saw that the men who came at me were themselves not free: it was not that cruelty was so sweet to them (though I am afraid sometimes it is), but that they didn't know what else to do. Even though they were white and hateful and my

---

[6] Charles Eagles, *Outsider Agitator* (Chapel Hill, N.C.: University of North Carolina Press, 1993) 62.

enemy, they were human beings, too. I found myself feeling a kind of grim affection for them, at least a love that was real and 'existential' rather than abstract...Last week in Camden I began to discover a new freedom in Christ: freedom to love the enemy. And in that freedom, the freedom to will and to try to set him free."[7]

The person who decided to eliminate Jonathan Daniels was Thomas Coleman. He was not known as a bad man, but rather a solid family man, a good neighbor, a churchman, and a loyal citizen. In fact, he made his living as a public employee, working for the county highway department. But apparently in his spare time he hung around the courthouse playing checkers. And listening to all the vile talk, the official rage, against the civil rights workers who had invaded their "peaceful" territory, where, under their claim, blacks and whites got along fine together. "The only good nigger is a dead nigger." "The worse white man is better than the best nigra." "You give these Negroes an inch and they'll take a mile." What the sheriff, the judge, the clerk of the court, and the lawyers constantly mouthed, this lowest of the lowest in the county bureaucracy, would take upon himself to correct. Whether it was a precipitous emotional act or the result of a long period of meditated malice we will never know. But observing the face and the actions of the young man studying for priesthood all of Coleman's own religious beliefs came into question. In his Sunday worship, God, the Bible, and Jesus were all mustered to undergird white supremacy and legal segregation. In Jonathan, he saw a "Christian" who defied segregation, who apparently enjoyed social life with the blacks, and who treated them as his equals. Coleman's religion was on trial, as well as his community's laws and customs. And since the ultimate test of religion is to kill or to be killed for one's god, Coleman took it upon himself to do what the "big shots" would not. When he raced from the courthouse where he

[7] Ibid., 64.

was playing dominoes to the Cash Store in the Negro part of town, did he envision himself as a new Atlas holding up the world of traditional white values? Looking at these four young people, two white boys and two black girls, all just a few minutes earlier having been released from the county jail in the courthouse, rushing to the store to buy some refreshments, Coleman was infuriated. Seeing these youths as they casually mixed, joking and laughing, enjoying life together without the slightest sense of embarrassment and shame, shook the foundations of Coleman's world. He jumped ahead of them to the door of the store and ordered them to stay out. When Jonathan protested about their rights, he pointed the shotgun he had brought with him at the pit of Jonathan's stomach and pulled the trigger. After having killed Jonathan, he turned his gun on the other white, who happened to be a Catholic priest, and seriously wounded him.

Coleman was no doubt convinced that he had done right and that he would win the favor of the entire white populace—that he was not in the least danger of being convicted of murder. His deed was largely seen as a good deed; he had done what others had not the courage to do. In the mock trial which followed, even the county prosecutor added falsified evidence in his summing up: he said, for example, that the store owner had authorized Coleman to close her store and that Daniels was "attempting to force his way in." The defense attorney declared in his summary, "These were not men of God as we know them here in Alabama." The jury deliberated for a total of one hour and thirty-one minutes to find Coleman "not guilty." The Reverend John Morris of the Episcopal Society for Cultural and Racial Unity, who had attended the entire proceedings, said: "We have witnessed an almost total conspiracy of the civil and religious leadership of Lowndes County to exonerate one of its own. Above all else, the most depressing part of this charade was the manner in which the church was trotted out in the person of local clergy, both on the stand and in the audience, to bless and announce absolution over the whole ritual of (Coleman's) absolution."[8]

After Daniels was murdered in Haynesville, the civil rights workers requested permission to hold a memorial service at St. Paul's Episcopal Church in Selma where Jonathan was a regular communicant. The Rector, T. Frank Matthews, rejected their request, and even though the rector received some denomination rebuke for his denial, his vestry promptly endorsed his decision. So instead, the following week leading bishops from across the nation, many friends of Jonathan, and crowds of local blacks filled Selma's Brown Chapel AME Church—where so many of Selma's periodic civil rights' rallies had been held—to celebrate Jonathan's life and witness.

---

[8] Ibid., 248.

CLARENCE JORDAN

One could hardly have found a more prototypical Southerner than Clarence Jordan, a Deep South Southerner at that—born in a small county-seat town in middle Georgia where his father was the banker, educated with an agriculture major at the University of Georgia, and never outside of the state except for the few years he was pursuing his doctorate at the Southern Baptist Theological Seminary in Louisville. And in religion he was out and out Baptist, which meant he took the Bible seriously (in maturity he preached with a well-worn Greek New Testament in his hand), was suspicious of the state, and preferred church-centeredness to social solutions. Like Martin Luther King Jr., he remained primarily a preacher until his death.

Sometime early in his career, he broke with his culture religion and, although white and with white supremist attitudes, customs and institutions dominating his world, he turned his back on that world and found a new philosophy, one that virtually agreed with King's without the two ever having crossed paths. (Except for one time, when King was jailed in Albany and Clarence traveled there to intercede with Police Chief Laurie Prichett to have King moved to a nearby town because of fear that King might be lynched.) Whereas King dreamed of a Beloved Community, Clarence and a few others established one, in 1942, called "Koinonia," after the New Testament Greek word for "participating love." Whereas

King's goal was integration, Clarence and the members of Koinonia began from the outset living together, black and white, twenty-four hours a day, seven days a week. Whereas King's method was non-violent, direct action, Jordan's group practiced a total pacifism that they saw as a realistic answer to humanity's warring madness. Moreover, in their community, they insisted on re-enacting the New Testament pattern of the church that according to their reading of the Book of Acts incorporated "community of goods." Within twenty-five years, Clarence would utilize the Hebrew "Jubilee" concept, where every fifty years the land would be redistributed, to start the Fund for Humanity which in turn spawned Habitat Humanity to build housing for the poor.

As soon as Koinonia was started, near Plains, Georgia (where lived another young man destined to become President of the United States, namely Jimmy Carter), it attracted unfavorable attention. How could it avoid drawing criticism with such "goings-on?" A preacher in overalls without a congregation? Practicing race-mixing? Refusing to enlist in the military? Living in bare-bones poverty at mere subsistence level? What Clarence conceived as scientific farming to renew the land, as a model for the impoverished black and white farmers surrounding them, their neighbors viewed as a bunch of idiots, or at their best, "those strange folks at Koinonia." Koinonia began on acreage that resembled the thousands of other run-down, hardscrabble farms throughout the South that had been ruined by King Cotton, the one-crop farming that had thoroughly depleted the original rich loam of the region. The naked red soil with its washed out gullies streaking the landscape gave the impression of a wounded, bleeding earth. The unpaved road which cut through their four hundred acres was virtually nonnegotiable in the mud of the winter and perennially dusty in the summer. On this poor, isolated, unpromising plot, Clarence dreamed not of a Civil Rights Movement but of a "Kingdom of God Movement."

What the Koinonians visualized as a model of interracial harmony, the white population saw as a threat to their way of life, a violation of their sacred taboos. Their opposition began slowly but reached a crescendo with the 1954 Supreme Court decision to desegregate the public schools. Their opposition used the churches, the businesses in an economic boycott, the Klan, an extended investigation by the County Grand Jury, a visit by the Chamber of Commerce leaders, and eventually the arrests and jailing of Koinonia members, the harassment of their children at school—even to the point of preventing their attendance-, the accusations that Koinonia was a communist center, and finally the almost daily acts of violence—burnings, bombings, vandalism, shootings from passing cars and the beatings inflicted on individual members. Things got so bad that Dr. Jordan abandoned his ideological stance against government aid and dispatched a telegram on 22 January 1957, appealing to President Eisenhower: "A community of nearly sixty men, women, and children is facing annihilation unless quick, decisive action is taken by someone in authority. I am therefore appealing to you as a last resort, with the hope and prayer that you might find some course of action before it is too late." He ended his long list of violent acts against Koinonia with these words: "We shall not run, for this is America. It is a land where free men have the right—and the duty—to walk erect and without fear in their pursuit of peace and happiness. Should this freedom perish from our land we would prefer to be dead. We gladly offer our lives for its preservation."[1] (The White House referred this telegram to the Attorney General of Georgia, one of the primary sources of Koinonia's persecution.)

---

[1] Contained in Jordan's FBI files (March 13, 1957, No. 144-1617-269).

Strangely—yet not too unthinkable since the churches were the guarantors of the white culture—the church people struck first. In early 1950, Dr. Jordan, his wife and children and other members of Koinonia were ousted from the local church just a mile or two down the road from the farm, the Rehoboth Baptist Church. Then the Klan began their attacks. First, with verbal threats and cross-burnings. On Sunday, 24 February 1957, a motorcade of some eighty cars filled with Ku-Klux-Klan drove slowly by the farm. A Koinonia mother pushing her baby carriage looked in amazement at the parade and, thinking someone had died, enquired of a driver, "Whose funeral?" The man replied gruffly, "It might as well be yours."[2] The Klansmen remained anonymous, but politicians locally and at the state level brazenly condemned Jordan and Koinonia. The Sumter County Solicitor, Charles Burgamy, declared at a political gathering, "May be that's what we need now for the right kind of Klan to start up again and use a buggy whip on some of these race mixers."[3]

Although Jordan and Koinonians in general did not participate directly in the Civil Rights moment—preferring, as Jordan put it, "to march every day integrated—, they publicly supported King, and during his Albany campaign, they housed the civil rights workers who found the social climate of Albany too inhospitable to remain in town over-night.

The questionable role of the FBI under its Director J. Edgar Hoover, has been brought to light in numerous studies of the Civil Rights Movement. Whereas civil rights workers had assumed they could appeal to the FBI for protection, in many cases they discovered instead that they were the victims of FBI cooperation with local authorities hounding them. Nowhere is this more evident than in the FBI surveillance of Clarence Jordan over a

---

[2] Dallas Lee, *The Cotton Patch Evidence* (N.Y.: Harper and Row, 1971) 125.
[3] Ibid., 112.

twenty-year period from 1948 to 1969, the year of his death. In the hundreds of pages of Jordan's FBI files I secured under the Freedom of Information Act, this conclusion is overwhelmingly corroborated. One instance will suffice. Dozens of pages are devoted to one particular Sunday in August, 1969, titled "Integrated Group Attending Church Services in Americus, Georgia." It deals with Jordan attempting to attend worship in the First Methodist Church. The FBI, apparently so disturbed by this "subversive, un-American act," not only had its agents alerted, but also notified the following "security" forces: the U.S. Secret Service of Atlanta; the III Military Intelligence Group of Fort McPherson, Georgia; the Police Department of Sumter County; the Georgia Bureau of Investigation; the United States Attorney of Macon, Georgia; the Naval Investigative Service Office of Charleston; and the Office of Special Investigation of Robins Air Force Base. What was the heinous, alarming offense? According to the Atlanta Office report, dated 25 August 1969, "On August 24, Clarence Jordan...had attempted to attend the First Methodist Church service and was accompanied by a Negro man and a Negro teenager." The agent further reported, "The personnel of the First Methodist Church would not allow the Negroes to enter. Because of this, Jordan refused to attend the church service but remained outside the church throughout the church service and at the completion of the church service attempted to talk with the members of the church as they were leaving." [4] This carefully documented and thoroughly cross-witnessed FBI surveillance report is probably the last public record of Clarence Jordan before he died. It is a tribute to a life lived unafraid of the consequences of opposing his culture in order to practice universal brotherhood.

---

[4] Contained in Jordan's FBI files (August 25, 1969, No. 157-3857).

RALPH ALLEN AND ZEV AELONY

Clarence Jordan and Koinonia Farm members chose not to participate directly in the Civil Rights Movement, which meant that they did not take to the streets with the Blacks in their campaign of protest against segregation laws. However, from its beginning in 1942 they practiced total integration within the life of their fellowship, day in and day out. But during the nearby city of Albany protests of 1962, initiated at first by the SNCC leader, Charles Sherrod, and later making national headlines with King's coming to town to assist them, Koinonia provided shelter for many of the protest leaders. They drove back and forth for the night and sometimes remained for longer periods to regroup and refresh themselves from the long and bitter-fought campaign. Nearly two thousand protesters were arrested over a two year period. On the night of 8 August 1963, two of the SNCC workers residing at Koinonia, Ralph Allen and John Purdue, were arrested and jailed for the next four months. They were charged under an old Georgia law against "inciting insurrection" (under which there was no possibility of bail).

Allen, a Texan, smuggled a letter out of the Sumter County jail which chronicled the circumstances of his arrest: "Police began to wade into the crowd of demonstrators with clubs, driving them back down the street with me, while someone in plain clothes stood firing a pistol in the air...Then the city marshal charged me from across the street and hit me a couple of times on the back and shoulders...I then noticed another white SNCC worker, John Purdue, as the marshal attacked him. After beating Purdue up...he came after me and hit me twice on the head with a billy club... Then he said, 'When I say run, you'd better run, you nigger-lovin' son-of-a-bitch...' My head was streaming blood."[1] A week later Zev Aelony, a Jewish CORE worker, was arrested under the same capital crime charge. Young blacks in Sumter County corresponded with them while they were in jail. One Americus girl wrote Allen: "White boy, only a fool would leave his heaven on earth just to fight for undeserving Negroes." Allen responded: "I do not understand, Gloria. It's no heaven on earth I left...Depends on what you mean by heaven. If you mean a place were everyone has so much money they have no sensitivity—no love, no sym-pathy, and no hope beyond their own narrow little worlds...Well, Gloria, I hope we can upset people enough to make them human."[2]

Zev Aelony felt so down, heated by the months of his imprisonment—constantly harassed by his fellow prisoners as a "nigger lover"—that he wrote his "last will and testament," which was smuggled out on a crumpled piece of brown wrapping paper and addressed to Koinonia: "Though there is now no immediate threat, there have been challenges to fight and the danger will probably recur. I won't hit back under any circumstance. I want so badly to live and to get out of here, but if I am killed, perhaps I can still dry some tears and bring some joy. If I die, please see to it that my eyes or any other organs or parts of my body that can be used for transplants or other medical uses are donated to those uses. Then, please, bury what's left of my body as it is without any box or coffin or any of that stuff, or embalming or fancy clothes other

---

[1] Howard Zinn, *SNCC: The New Abolitionists* (Boston: Beacon Press, 1964) 183.
[2] Ibid., 184.

than what happens to be on the body, and then bury it at Koinonia. Just please plant a tree, a plum or a fig or a peach or a pecan, something that bears sweet fruit and has a long life, so that it may use what remains of my body to make pleasures for children of my brothers here in Sumter County. Please see to it that no revenge or punishment or prosecution is taken against those of my brothers who have struck me down, but only that Sumter County officials be enjoined from putting a man ever again, no matter what heinous crime accused, in the exposed position I'm in here. Thank you so much. May you all be blessed."[3] After four months of prison, a three-judge federal court ruled unconstitutional the Georgia statute under which they had been held, and the three of them were released.

---

[3] Clarence Jordan, *Cotton Patch Sermons.* Editor Dallas Lee (N.Y.: Association Press, 1972) 76.

CONRAD BROWNE

Conrad Browne spent fourteen years of his life at Koinonia Farm near Americus, Georgia—a Christian commune dedicated to interracial brotherhood, peace, and economic sharing. The years were from 1949 to 1963 from soon after his marriage till he left to assume the assistant directorship of the Highlander Folk School in Tennessee. When he departed the Farm, he reported that there were 132 bullet-holes in the house they had lived in—from shots fired from the roadway by white supremacists intent on destroying the Farm and chasing away all its residents. From the time Koinonia was founded in 1942 and the subsequent twenty years covering the time of Browne's residence, the Farm had generated hostility from its white neighbors because of its interracial practices. But over the years, as the Farm members taught Christian acceptance of blacks on equal terms at the local Baptist church, as they championed the cause of equality of education and with the Supreme Court decision on desegregating the public schools in 1954 the endorsing of that legal mandate, as they insisted on equal pay to black and white farm laborers, and as they housed the civil rights workers from the near-by Albany protests, they came under heavy fire, fire which was quite literal: dynamiting their road-side stand, setting fire to their barns, and almost nightly firing of guns at the residences and members of the Farm.

All shootings were reported to police in town. A sheriff came to investigate, but only long enough to look at the outside of the house shot into. Nothing developed from the investigation, nor from any of the endless reports which Koinonia members registered with the law authorities. The violence lasted for more than a decade—beatings, bombings, burnings, boycotting, and bullets. On top of that, the local school decided to ban Koinonia children from attending. They had to appeal to the Federal Circuit Court to issue an order admitting their children to the public school. Afterwards Browne's children were constantly harassed by name-calling, acid throwing, destruction of their science fair exhibits, and shunning.

Browne has recorded one such personal episode.

> I was delivering boxes of pecans from the Farm for shipment at the Railway Express in Americus. A man with brass knuckles hit me in the face several times, knocking me into the front seat of my truck. When the Express agent came out, the man ran. The agent soaked up my bleeding with a paper towel. He accompanied me to a doctor, who sewed me up and sent me home. Hardly had I gotten to bed when the Sheriff appeared and arrested me. He took me to the County Jail on the charge that I 'was beating my head on the curb to gain public notice,' a charge that carried a $64.00 fine and court costs. There was a lockup tank. Only two of us were there that night, the other being a huge black man. Immediately he began eyeing my watch. 'Man, that's the purtiest watch I've ever seen.' I told him he could have it, and I took it off and gave it to him. That started an all night conversation during which he poured out to me his life-record of stealing and murder. I fell asleep from my heavy medication and

awoke the next morning to find my cell-mate gone but my watch was laying on my chest.[1]

That was the manner in which the Koinonians responded to the violence perpetrated by the larger community, mostly aroused by their intense and deep-rooted prejudice against whites who broke with the white supremacist culture and who sided with the blacks in their campaign for civil rights.

---

[1] Quotations and facts provided by Conrad Browne to the author in September 1999 (notes and personal interview).

HOWARD KESTER

Howard Kester, who died in 1977, spent his life disturbing Southern mores by his work in the peace movement, in labor organizing—especially among the black tenants of the Delta—and in interracial activities. A Christian minister born in Virginia, he was a freelancer, spurning the institutional church as too timid but associating himself with such religious experiments as Highlander Folk School (Tennessee), Providence Farm (Mississippi), Penn Community (South Carolina) and the Fellowship of Southern Churchmen (headquartered at first in Chapel Hill but ending its years at its Buckeye Cove grounds in western North Carolina). It is his executive directorship with the latter that he is most noted for. In 1934, Kester and two other young Southern ministers, James Dombrowski and Myles Horton envisioned an organization which would bring together Christians of the South who promoted the social application of the Gospel. On 4 December about forty ministers from over the Southland gathered at the Third Presbyterian Church in Chattanooga, Tennessee, and thus began the FSC. Its goals were threefold: to assist the neediest—sharecroppers, textile workers and the unemployed—, to lead the fight against Jim Crowism, and to develop a biblical message of social justice. It established a magazine, *Prophetic Religion*, and it began the first "race-mixing" in the South, such as the summer interracial camps it sponsored and in its own periodic gatherings. In its first public statement, it declared:

> We condemn the manifest injustices to the Negro, as evidenced in discrimination by employers and trade unions in the matter of wages, in the exclusion from skilled trades and in the courts, in the disproportionate sums expended for education, in restricting the right of suffrage, in the operation of Jim Crow laws, and the inadequacy of housing, recreation, and health facilities. We call upon church groups to make the principle of brotherhood concrete in the relationships between the races.[1]

They knew they had taken on a risky task but they were undaunted in their youthful vision. The continuing public opposition to their innovations continued throughout the duration of the FSC. For instance, in the summer of 1947, at an FSC work camp in eastern North Carolina that was engaged in building a cannery in a black community, the participants were chased by a white mob into the surrounding cornfields. A Charlotte paper reported: "An interracial church group living in the home of a Negro in defiance of segregation customs was ordered out of Tyrell County...by a group of more than 300 white people who gave them twenty-four hours to leave."[2]

Kester did occasional assignments for the national office of the NAACP, which included hastening to any reported lynching and gathering concrete evidence on the perpetrators. This was without saying dangerous "spying," and he oftentimes escaped with just his life. One night in 1936, he drove from Memphis to a meeting in a church near Parkin, Arkansas, a meeting called to protest the shooting of black sharecroppers by county deputies the night

---

[1] Anthony Dunbar, *Against the Grain* (Charlottesville: University of Virginia Press, 1981) 61.

[2] Ibid., 230.

before. Kester had barely reached the pulpit when a squad of men armed with ax handles and guns broke into the building and began clubbing the people in the pews. They waded through the church, striking and cursing anybody they could reach. Some of the sharecroppers escaped through the church windows, taking glass and sash with them, but Kester continued with his speech. What kept him in the pulpit, he said, was the example of a group of black women seated directly in front of him who refused to acknowledge the mayhem to their rear. Soon, however, there was no one left but these few and the mob, whose leader strode up to Kester demanding, "Are you coming peaceably or will we have to take you?" Kester replied, "I am breaking no law, and if you want me you will have to take me." Whereupon they did, forcing the feisty preacher from the pulpit and out of the church. They sat him behind the wheel of his own '32 Chevrolet, put two gunmen on the running boards, and ordered him to follow their lead car out of town.

Kester was taken through the darkened streets of Earle. Once he had to slow abruptly to avoid hitting a small dog. The gunman beside him snarled, "You care more about dogs than you do about white people," but Kester reflected that he would have given pretext for an even angrier outburst had he hit the dog. Past Earle, they took a dirt road into the woods and halted. The captive was pulled from his car and a hangman's nose dangled before his eyes.

Kester summoned all his persuasive powers and began speaking loudly to one of the leaders of the gang, a man he recognized as an Earle cotton broker. He had harmed no one, Kester pointed out, and since he was not from Arkansas his murder would be investigated by federal authorities. The abductors could be identified by scores of people back at the church and were sure to be convicted. The kidnappers drew aside for a private discussion, but Kester overheard the words, "This man is telling the truth. We could get in a pack of trouble." The broker put an end to the talk by saying he had decided to escort Kester to the Mississippi River Bridge into Tennessee, but that if he ever returned to Arkansas, "We'll shoot you on sight." Kester drove the twenty-five miles back to the river, and across it, in a cold sweat.

Meanwhile, union members had carried the word to Memphis that Kester had been captured and likely lynched. They called the local Associated Press bureau chief, who relayed the news to New York City. It was soon told to Norman Thomas, who was addressing a meeting at the Hotel Roosevelt. Thomas sadly announced the fate of his friend, and shortly several listeners were sending telegrams of condolence to Alice in Nashville. It was not until several hours later, after her husband had collected his wits and found a telephone, that Alice learned he was still alive. Howard drove to Nashville that night, reaching home around 4 o'clock in the morning. He and his wife spent the remaining hours of darkness huddled together in front of the fireplace, Alice weeping.[3]

MYLES HORTON

Myles Horton was not ashamed throughout his life to be known as "a hill-billy" from the mountains of east Tennessee, where he was born in 1905. And, no matter how many trips he made outside of Appalachia throughout America and overseas, he remained fixed to his region. First going to college there, Cumberland, then in 1932, in the mountains west of Chattanooga, in one of America's poorest counties, putting his dreams into reality with the establishment of Highlander Folk School. He had dreamed up the "folk school" while studying them in Denmark in 1931. From his diary there: "The school will be for young men and women of the mountains and workers from factories. Negroes will be among the students who will live in close personal contact with the teacher. Out of their experiential learning through living, working, and studying together could come understanding of how to take their place intelligently in the changing world."[1] When Horton wrote down this vision, he had no idea that the word "integration" would become in the next decades the fighting concept of his region, that Highlander would be a major center of its instrumentation, and that he would personally face jail and be physically beaten for endorsing the term. Yet, already in his days in college and afterwards as a State of Tennessee student YMCA secretary, he had

---

[1] Myles Horton, *The Long Haul* (N.Y.: Doubleday Publishers, 1990) 54.

faced the problem of racial segregation and had defied it. "We had interracial meetings all over the state...I didn't ask anybody anything; I just did it...through no great idealism. It was just that I didn't want to be segregated. As a mountaineer I was segregated from people who weren't mountaineers...as a country boy I was segregated from city people...I didn't like any kind of segregation...I never thought of it as race...I just don't believe in segregation, I don't care what it is."[2] For the school year 1929-30 Norton enrolled at Union Theological Seminary where the radical socialist theologian, Reinhold Niebuhr, appealed to Horton's way of thinking. That was a critical move because when he returned from Denmark in 1932, Niebuhr, along with his friends, Sherwood Eddy, Norman Thomas, and Kirby Page contributed the sum of $1,300 toward his projected folk school. With the help of a local resident, Dr. Lillian Johnson, who turned over to Horton her house at Monteagle, Tennessee, what was to become famous throughout the South—Highlander—was born. From its statement of purpose: "We hold that democracy is inactive unless workers are given a full voice in industry; or farmers are given a voice in the marketplace through cooperatives; or where freedom of thought and discussion is limited; that democracy is outlawed by legally entrenched discrimination and segregation."

When Highlander came under fire from Southern conservative political leaders in the 1950s, it was not all the other educational activities it had sponsored which drew attention. It was their "race-mixing." The opposition fixed on its Labor Day weekend of 1957 when some 200 black and white leaders from across the South convened at Highlander. Among the speakers was Aubrey Williams, former president of the Southern Conference of Human Welfare, and Martin Luther King Jr. Governor Marvin Griffin of

---

[2] Thomas Bledsoe, *Or We'll All Hang Separately* (Boston: Beacon Press, 1969) 36.

Georgia took it upon himself to lead the attack by distributing 250,000 copies of a brochure accusing Highlander of being communist-supported and featuring the now-famous photograph of King alongside a known communist (who had surreptitiously enrolled and deliberated staged the photo juxtaposition). It read in part: "They met at this workshop and discussed methods and tactics of precipitating racial strife and disturbance. The meeting of such a large group of specialists in interracial strife under the auspices of a Communist Training School, and in the company of many known Communists is the typical method whereby leadership training and tactics are furnished to the agitators..."[3] The facts contained in the brochure were all skewed: what was indeed true were the many training sessions that had been held at Highlander by civil rights leaders. Probably its most famous "graduate" was Rosa Parks, who on 1 December 1955 had refused to move from the white section of a Montgomery, Alabama, bus. She later wrote of her experiences at Highlander before that event: "At Highlander, I found out for the first time in my adult life that this could be a unified society, that there was such a thing as people of differing races and backgrounds, meeting together in workshops and living together in peace and harmony. It was a place I was very reluctant to leave. I gained there strength to persevere in my work for freedom, not just for blacks but all oppressed people."[4] Governor Griffin's salvo was followed in 1959 by an investigative hearing staged by the Tennessee Legislature "to expose Highlander's communist connections." On 12 March the hearing committee recommended the revocation of the school's charter, which was enacted by a court injunction. As a result, Attorney General Albert Sloan padlocked Highlander's main

---

[3] Frank Adams, *Unearthing Seeds of Fire* (Winston Salem, N.C.: John F. Blair Publishers, 1975), 125.
[4] Ibid., 122.

building. Horton, speaking from makeshift quarters, said, "You can padlock a building. But you can't padlock an idea. Highlander is an idea. You can't kill it and you can't close it in." Later, on July 31, 1959 Sloan led a massive law officers' raid onto the grounds of Highlander. On the pretense that they were "drunk," several staff members were jailed overnight. Horton happened to be away on a speaking engagement. However general public hostility was so intense and continuous that Highlanders were constantly in danger. Horton, while eating at a restaurant in Maryville with his lawyer, Edward Lynch, was beaten. The public consensus was "anybody who believed in integration must be a communist."

While the government's highest authorities were pressuring Highlander, the local KKK was adding its part. In August 1960, the last group to utilize Highlander's facilities was the Student Nonviolent Coordinating Committee. Nightriders attacked the school firing into the buildings, narrowly missing Stokeley Carmichael. Ultimately, Horton's "integrationist" stance brought down the operation of the school. In the fall 1960 trial, the Attorney General charged, among the nine points of the indictment, that Highlander "violated an old Tennessee law forbidding whites and Negroes to attend classes together." During the trial, the prosecution "played around with all the charges (introducing the integration issue more covertly and by constant innuendo rather than overtly)..." Attorney General Sloan "injected race again and again without being too specific. Reference had been made to Septima Clark (the main adult counselor of the SNCC gathering). He pointed to her in the audience to make sure everyone saw she was a Negro. 'Why she's a big ramrod out at Highlander.' (Then) he passed around the Gov. Griffin still picture of the folk dance where a white woman and a Negro were caught close together."[5]

---

[5] Ibid., 138.

Realizing they could no longer operate at their Monteagle site, Highlander purchased property within the city of Knoxville and moved there in 1961. Although they found Knoxville slightly more accepting of their school, public wrath seemed to mount. In June 1963, one of their North-South work camps, where about two dozen black and white students were erecting a community building on private property, was raided. Led by the sheriff of the county, the posse struck at 3:00 A.M.; all the camp's participants were herded to the county jail at Maryville where they were charged the next day with "disorderly conduct, lewdness, possession of alcohol, and contributing to the delinquency of minors." Such assaults reached their peak between 1965 and 1968. Staff members endured a storm of adverse publicity in the *Knoxville Journal*, a Ku Klux Klan parade pass the center, repeated vandalism, firebombs, burglaries, gunshots, and taped telephone messages branding Highlander as a "malignant organization" whose "red spiders" taught "hate, violence and riots." Another attempt was launched in the state legislature to have their second charter revoked. However nothing came of this move, and by 1970, with its lessened role in the Civil Rights Movement, Highlander found itself concentrating on the needs of Appalachia. Myles Horton resigned as director that year, but continued his role as senior consultant.

VIRGINIA DURR

"The worst time of all, to me, was 1961, the year of the Freedom Rides....I felt absolute terror. I'd lived in Montgomery for ten years. We'd gone through the bus boycott and the Brown decision and all the things that had happened after the Brown decision. We'd gone through the Eastland hearing. What terrified me so was that the people who were shouting and holding up their babies to 'see the niggers run' were just ordinary Montgomery people who had come downtown on Saturday as they usually do to shop. And they had turned into a raving mob. It was a terrifying sight...These were people I was living among and they were really crazy. They were full of hatred and they were full of bigotry and meanness. They were enjoying the sight of these Negroes and these white students being beat up. I didn't face the mob, because I was on the second story of the building across the street. But it was pretty terrifying all the same."[1]

Virginia Durr was in her sixties at the time, having lived in the South all her years (her father was a Presbyterian pastor in Birmingham) and her marriage to Clifford Durr, a lawyer practicing during the 1950s in Montgomery, had produced five children. She had been reared the proper "Southern belle," but

---

[1] Virginia Durr, *Outside the Magic Circle* (Tuscaloosa: University of Alabama Press, 1990) 297.

sometime in midlife she had altered course radically. First, she became a national leader to abolish the poll tax, a device used by the post-Reconstruction South to prevent blacks from voting. In doing so, she discovered such women's groups as the Women's Society for Christian Service (Methodist), the United Church Women (ecumenical), Mrs. M. E. Tilly's Atlanta-based Women Against Lynching and the Women's International League for Peace and Freedom—she found that the Southern women aligned with these groups were her best allies. Her brother-in-law was on the US Supreme Court, Hugo Black, also from Alabama. All these connections, along with her husband's high ranking job in the Roosevelt New Deal, opened her eyes to a new world view.

So it is not too surprising that Virginia Durr, a prominent Montgomery citizen, should have had a hand in Rosa Parks' historic stand (sit-down in the public bus on 1 December 1955 that originated the Montgomery Improvement Association led by Martin Luther King Jr.). Myles Horton, director of Highlander Folk School, contacted Virginia about potential enrollees for his summer school in civil rights. Virginia approached her friend, Rosa Parks, paid for her bus fare to Tennessee, and even gave Rosa a swim suit for her recreational use while there. All this happened the summer before December 1955. When Rosa was arrested and jailed for her disobeying the Jim Crow law, Virginia's husband was requested by Mrs. Parks' black lawyer to intercede with the court officials. Virginia accompanied her husband to the jail: "I waited for them while they made bail. Everything went smoothly. They brought Mrs. Parks out from behind the bars. That was a terrible sight to me to see this gentle, lovely, sweet woman, whom I knew and was so fond of, being brought down by a matron....We all went to her apartment, and after she had freshened up and had a little supper, Cliff and Mr. Nixon (her lawyer) and Mrs. Parks and her husband and her mother and I discussed the case."[2] From that inconspicuous beginning originated the Civil Rights Movement of the 1950s, and Mrs. Parks' case eventually was handled favorably by the US Supreme Court. It also instantly made the Durr's infamous in their home locale.

But already Virginia's good Southern standing was in jeopardy. US Senator Jim Eastland was on the Senate's Judiciary Committee and he was chairman of the Internal Security Subcommittee. In March 1954, Eastland decided to hold public hearings in New Orleans "to root out subversives." Virginia was subpoenaed to appear before that hearing. "Southerners knew instinctively that Eastland's attack on me was aimed at the Supreme Court and the Brown decision and Hugo Black."[3] She found herself smeared as a "communist" simply for holding liberal views on the race issue—a common misappropriation throughout the South, but a very effective political tool to discredit challengers to the Southern way of life. She weathered that storm by defying Senator Eastland's tactics and, thereby, won considerable media attention, even general national admiration. But the domestic cost was considerable. "A lot of people who had been coming to our law office (she worked as legal secretary to her husband) about wills and deeds dropped away. We had never had a big practice, but what we had began to slide away....The situation was hard on the children....One of Tilla's teachers told her in front of the class, 'You just tell your uncle I'm not going to teach any nigger children. I don't care how many laws they pass.' Well, that was a hard thing for a child of twelve or thirteen to take. Tilla, from that point on, hated the school and wanted to get out of it."[4] Lula, the youngest and in the first grade, was refused admission to the home of her

[2] Ibid., 280.
[3] Ibid., 269.
[4] Ibid., 269.

friend's birthday party. "Our lives changed drastically as a result of the Eastland hearing....We didn't know whether we would be attacked or whether there'd be crosses burned. ....The Eastland hearing had an effect on Cliff, too. When the Brown decision came down in 1954, all hell broke loose. There was no choice. You either had to stand up and be counted or move. We didn't move."[5]

Virginia's United Church Women decided to hold their first integrated gathering, an all-day meeting with lunch. The leader of the White Citizens organization took down all the license numbers of the cars at the meeting. He published the names and telephone numbers and addresses of everybody in his paper, "Sheet Lightning." The women listed began receiving harassing telephone calls at night and were threatened in other ways. "By the time of the Regal Cafe case, living in Montgomery was like living in the midst of a storm. You never knew what was going to happen. We worried for the black people and for ourselves, but mostly we worried for our children."[6] The Regal Cafe case pertained to a touring group of white college students from a Methodist institution in Jacksonville, Illinois. Led by their dean, they had come to Montgomery to investigate the civil rights protests. They had gone with an accompanying group of Alabama State Teachers' College students to this black restaurant known as the Regal Cafe. The city fathers had backed away from declaring integration illegal but they had passed an ordinance that if anyone did anything that was likely to provoke a breach of peace, that person would be arrested on a criminal offense. While the students were sitting in the cafe with the dean and his wife and their three-year-old daughter, the police raided the cafe and arrested them all. Mr. and Mrs. Durr went to the jail but they couldn't raise enough money for the bail (as there were too many students), but they did raise

---

[5] Ibid., 271-2.
[6] Ibid., 292.

bail for the dean and his wife. Meanwhile, when placed in the jail, their three-year-old child had been seized by the police and placed under foster care. The Durrs worked frantically all night to find the infant and get it returned to its parents. Judge Lowe presided at the police court the next day and all were found guilty. For two years, Lawyer Durr appealed the case through federal courts and finally got the conviction overturned in *Nesmith v. Alford* by the Fifth Court of Appeals in New Orleans.

Virginia's husband taught a Sunday school class at the prestigious First Presbyterian Church of Montgomery, where several generations of Durrs had been pillars of the congregation. One Sunday after his name had been heralded in the press as the defense lawyer for these civil rights cases, he entered the classroom to discover not a single member of his class was present. That was their signal that they never wanted to listen to him again. Still the Durrs refused to move their residence and their legal office out of Montgomery. Were they ostracized? Yes. Were they harassed? Yes. Their Buick automobile was burned by a street mob. Were they scared? Yes. Virginia frankly confesses in her autobiography: "But mostly I was scared for myself, if you want to know the honest-to-God truth. I just felt that I would live and die with people who could be absolute brutes, and how did I know that they wouldn't turn on me? It was a terrifying time. I still have nightmares about it sometimes."[7]

---

[7] Ibid., 299.

DAVID MINTER

Holmes County, Mississippi, where Providence Farm was located, is on the edge of the Delta about sixty miles south of Oxford. In 1955, it was one of the poorest counties in the United States, and as late as 1993 it was still ranked fifth from the bottom. Providence was founded in the 1930s to assist the poor tenant farmers, both white and black, though the latter composed two thirds of the population of the county. It provided a cooperative grocery, a credit union, a supplemental school for black children and a medical clinic. Dr. David Minter, a Texan, came right out of medical school in 1938 and opened his clinic in a renovated dairy barn. The Presbyterian Board of Missions guaranteed him a salary the first year of up to one thousand dollars. That year he took in $994.

When, by happenstance, I visited the Farm in the fall of 1955 it was under siege by the White Citizen Council of the county—completely unbeknownst to me and Will Campbell, my traveling companion. (I had been the principal speaker at an University of Mississippi convocation that morning and had asked Will, the chaplain, to drive me down to see friends whom I knew to work there. My friends were Dr. Minter and his wife, Sue Wooten, their three children, and Gene Cox, his wife, and their children.) At a mass meeting at Tchula High School a few weeks before, prompted by White Citizen Council leaders—assembled like a kangaroo court—they were ordered to disband and the families were told to leave the county. For the moment, they were living through days of terror, telephone lines cut, fire insurance on their houses suspended because of burning threats, and roadblocks stopping all incoming traffic manned by county sheriff deputies. By sheer good luck, we had been told in Tchula by the country doctor how to slip in the back way. Rarely have I seen on all my investigations of human rights violations such frightened faces on the victims of public terrorism. Will and I could not believe this scene was happening in America. And, to our own unease, it dawned upon us that now that we were "insiders," we could be labeled as accomplices to their crime.

And what was their "crime?" According to the proceedings of the "kangaroo" court convened on 27 September 1955 it was "race-mixing." There was no question that for nearly two decades these white families had lived with and ministered to the black population—a fact that was public knowledge, especially to the local Durant Presbyterian Church where the families attended weekly services. In fact, the question that perennially bugged the citizens of the county was "why would any doctor stick himself away in such an obscure place?" When the question was put to Dr. Minter again that night, Dr. Minter's answer still didn't satisfy. "It's the kind of thing I like to do. I am motivated by religious conviction to heal body, soul and mind." (They could accept the fact that his brother was missionary to Africans in Nigeria—paid for by some of their own church giving—, but not that he could be "a missionary" to blacks in Holmes County!)

The prime movers of the Tchula High School assemblage were all three presidents of local chapters of the White Citizens Council: County Attorney Pat Barrett of the Lexington chapter, State Representative J. P. Love of the Tchula chapter, and local businessman, William Moses, of the County chapter. The two characteristics words known for decades to describe the Farm, "interracial" and "cooperative," were now anathema to these leaders—incendiary words for people long devoted and committed to what they knew as the 'Southern way of life.' Both words were sure to pique the passions of those persuaded already by their own history that God was the original segregationist, and reinforced by the years of Senator Joe McCarthy's preachments that a communist conspiracy was behind every effort to destroy ancient customs. The long afternoon session at the school house grew angrier and angrier—Cox declared the night we were visiting, "I believe they would have killed us then if the children outside on the playground had not ended their ballgame and entered the auditorium to rejoin their parents."[1] Just before the vote to chase them from the County, State Representative Edwin White summoned up the mood. "We just can't afford to have them up here teaching what they are teaching...which will lead to violence unless it is stopped."[2]

What was not admissible by that assembly was the ominous reality that all the subsequent violence, for the next eight months until the two families could make arrangements to move elsewhere, was perpetrated against the dwellers of Providence Farm. At first, the Minters and the Coxes determined to defy the mandate to evacuate and continued to tend to their duties. But the increasing threats and the all-night "parties" consisting of rowdies at the borders of the Farm gave them a siege mentality. They couldn't sleep, the women and children lost their appetite and when the they did eat they were so nervous they vomited it up; they lived in constant fear day and night. Gene Cox was driven to

---

[1] Will Campbell, *Providence* (Atlanta, Georgia: Longstreet Press, 1992) 7, 14-15.

[2] Anthony Dunbar, *Against the Grain* (Charlottesville: University of Virginia Press, 1981) 244.

such desperation that, resolute pacifist though he was, he started carrying a loaded revolver, stuck in his belt, to defend themselves from would-be attackers. They lived without any outside support. The blockaders prevented any newsagents from entering to publicize their plight. The Farm members considered them neglected by the whole world.

Our surprise visit turned into a long, painful evening of trying to reassure them and of promising to get the word out. Will and I managed to "escape" late that night by passing through the road blockade. "Let us see your identification papers," the self-appointed security guards demanded. "Who are you?" they asked of Will, the driver, with a flashlight blinding his eyes. "I'm a Baptist preacher from Oxford." "And you?" they directed toward me. "I'm a Baptist preacher from Macon, Georgia." The posse must still be wondering how two Baptist preachers could have circumvented their roadblock, and, even more, how was it possible that two so inoffensive personages as preachers from their own south-land be involved in such regional espionage.

WILL CAMPBELL

Will Campbell, born in Mississippi, with degrees from Wake Forest University and Yale Divinity School, and ordained a Baptist minister, never intended to be a central figure in the Southern racial turmoil. But in the social climate that hardened in the South following the 1954 Supreme Court mandate to desegregate public schools, there was little choice left for the conscience sensitive to social justice. Just three choices: either one remained by the status quo of white supremacy or one made small gestures to change the system and became immediately known as an "integrationist" (and therefore a traitor to the region) or one sided with the communists, a small but vocal subgroup in the South. Unfortunately, the mindset of the Southern status quo linked integration and communism as if they were one cultural enemy. (The irony of identifying racial justice with communism is that it gave the edge over democracy and Christianity to those labeled as "aliens to the American Way.) What Campbell quickly discovered is that his own claim to Christianity was tainted by the fact that all three choices wrapped up their defense with the Christian label.

> His preaching/pastoring ministry began innocuously and unnoticed in a small sawmill village in Louisiana. Nobody paid much attention to his endorsing the Supreme Court decision as "the Christian thing to do." As he tells it, "[The local populace]

really didn't envision the possibility (of its enactment). The thought of black children going to school with their children was so outrageous that they just didn't see it as an eventuality. It was like somebody saying, 'Hey, you gonna die.' Well, you know, you are someday; so they said, 'Well, someday this might happen, but not in our time, so don't worry about it.' But Will did. "I'd preach on it about every other Sunday—not about the decision, but about race—and they thought it was kind of cute, you know: our little preacher, he's the cutest thing, he's talking about our children going to school with little darkies. He's so cute." But as the storm clouds gathered the local people were "beginning to not think that was so cute any more."[1]

Leaving the first and only parish he ever held, Campbell moved to the campus of the University of Mississippi to be director of religious life. He naively thought that "he could be an invaluable ally to the university which, he was sure, would draw on his enlightenment and liberalism as it moved to full equality." But once again, his conscientious choice between the three alternatives, even his slightest, timid move got him in trouble. Once Campbell was caught in the act of playing Ping Pong with a black person. "The dean said, 'You know, Will, I don't object, for God's sake. I'm from Columbus, Ohio; I've played Ping Pong with a black man—in my basement. But don't do it in public because, you know, you're just asking for trouble, and you've got to protect the institution."[2]

As word spread of Campbell's deviations from what the law called the 'established traditions, customs, and usages of the State of Mississippi,' reprisals began against him. His secretary told him that a law student came to Campbell's office every evening to

---

[1] Fred Powledge, *Free at Last* (Boston: Little, Brown and Co., 1991) 98.
[2] Ibid., 97.

collect carbons from the wastebasket. Campbell learned that the student took the carbons to his home and held them up against a lamp to see what the minister was writing. And at a social function hosted by Campbell, he discovered human excrement floating in the bowl containing the beverage.[3] With his association with the members of Providence Farm some ninety miles south of Oxford, which for the moment was under siege by the White Citizens Council, his tenure at Ole Miss came to an abrupt end.

Since then, the preacher-boy born on a farm in Mississippi has spent the latter half of his life on a farm in Tennessee, dividing his day between his log cabin study and the local tavern—the cabin where he generates his communications with the larger world and the tavern which serves as his surrogate church. For decades he has flourished as a "preacher without a steeple," busy exploding the racist mythos and exploring ways to overcome it. In 1957 he was at Little Rock High School protecting one of the black girls entering the school door. He was in Atlanta as the one white in the organizing session of King's Southern Christian Leadership Conference. In 1960 he shared the speakers' platform with Martin Luther King Jr. at the first national ecumenical conference on race. In his professional post as Executive Director of the Committee of Southern Churchmen (an extension of the Fellowship of Southern Churchmen founded in 1934 to link the isolated whites and blacks working together as equals) he traveled all over the South bringing aid and encouragement to persons victimized in the racial strife. In addition, he commenced his writing career: his first book being *Race and the Renewal of the Church*. Just about all his books since have indirectly dealt with the subject. As Campbell's name spread across the national news media, word came from back home in Mississippi that he would not be welcome to the usual funerals, weddings and holidays. As he put it in a recent interview, "There

---

[3] Ibid., 179.

was a conspiracy to kill me." The facts have gradually emerged over the years. "A young man who knew the elder Campbells had overheard his own father confessing tearfully to his mother that the decision had been made to kill Will Campbell. As the story was relayed to Tennessee, the informant had said, 'Papa was crying and about half drunk and was telling mama that he had to kill Will, and he was crying because he didn't want to.'"[4]

Speaking cavalierly and with the dry humor he has cultivated over the years of facing tense situations and violent antagonists, Campbell added: "There was no real personal hatred of me. It's like my little dog goes rabid, I have to take him out behind the barn and shoot him because he is a danger and a menace. You see, I'd gone rabid. I was a traitor to the community, to the South, to the family, and to the faith. I was a communist in their mind. They were going to kill me, really, out of a broken heart."[5]

---

[4] Jeremy Lloyd, "Radical Grace: An Interview with Will D. Campbell," *The Sun Magazine* (May 2000): 15.

[5] Powledge, *Free at Last*, 451.

CLAUDIA SANDERS

One of the least offensive documents on race relations was issued in October 1957. Entitled "South Carolinians Speak," it was sponsored by five of the state's leading clergymen and consisted of twelve testimonials by prominent citizens, men and women, across the state. Endorsing integration was not their collective goal, but what little they said in behalf of obeying the 1954 Supreme Court desegregation ruling was taken as that. On the night of 19 November less than a month after the pamphlet's publication, the home of one of its contributors was dynamited. Mrs. Claudia Thomas Sanders, the wife of a Gaffney physician and a native of Charleston, whose ancestry there went back to the city's earliest days, had made the statement in her contribution to the pamphlet, "Gradual desegregation in the schools accomplished by starting with the first grades would seem logical to me." She was a grandmother and the parent of two children. She was a member of the Episcopal Church of the Incarnation in Gaffney, the American Association of University Women, and the Home and Garden Club. As a prominent leader in her town, she served on the hospital auxiliary and the County Library Board. She had no political agenda, and made her appeal primarily based on her religious faith.

"As a follower of Christ I believe that God is my Father and that all men are my brothers," she began. She ended with the sentence,

"We must move surely because our social conscience and Christian ethics leave us no alternative." In between, she made the points that "no longer is it popular to propose one law for men and another for women, or even one for white and another for black....I want for my child and for every child of God the right to lift his eyes and to say within himself, 'There is a place for me in America, in South Carolina if I choose. There is work for my hands and brain. There is happiness and achievement waiting for me if I am true to the best that is within me.' I do not want the color of his skin to kill that dream or a lack of educational opportunity to place chains upon his spirit more terrible than the iron chains that shackled the limbs of his forebears." Then came her telling sentence: "First, the idea of desegregation must be accepted, then practical steps taken that will lead us to the desired results."[1]

For that, she was singled out by the white racists of the state for retribution. Her two-story house was rocked by an explosion that shattered windows all along the street, and left a gaping hole near the chimney. Had the unexploded time bomb—composed of three sticks of dynamite, a time clock, and a battery device—functioned as planned, death and injury to all the occupants of the house would have been certain. William Peters, a journalist taking note of the courageous Southern women who spoke up at this crucial moment, has written: "...Some of the most vociferous attacks of the segregationists are reserved not for the crusading Negroes or 'interfering' Northerners but for 'traitorous' Southern whites who abandon tradition and campaign openly for desegregation....It would appear that this is the point where Southern male chivalry ends, for the fact that a renegade Southerner is of the gentler sex provides no assurance that her punishment will be correspond-

[1] John Morris, ed., *South Carolinians Speak* (Dillon SC: Privately printed, 1957) 71-72.

ingly gentler."[2] Mrs. Sanders braved the brunt of Peter's general observation, and she had the courage to stick it out.

---

[2] William Peters, *The Southern Temper* (New York: Doubleday & Co., 1959) 28.

BOB ZELLNER

Bob Zellner was a homegrown prospect for the Civil Rights Movement. He had grown up in and around Montgomery, Alabama, and entered the local Methodist college, Huntingdon, just as King's bus boycott was in full swing. The critical question is why, of all the bright white college students in similar circumstances across the South—in Nashville, Greensboro, Danville, Tallahassee, Jackson, Birmingham, and other hot spots—was he the rare candidate to commit himself wholeheartedly to the cause? Let him present his own raison d'etre:

> My father's father was a Klansman...But dad was a thinking person and a real dedicated Christian and as he got older he just could not make his Klanism and his Christianity jive. One of the reasons I was a little bit different from my peers is we were poor. My mother was a school teacher and my daddy was a preacher and there were five boys in the family...He always was the circuit rider preacher with six, seven, sometimes twelve churches, mostly in the country.
>
> In my senior year in college we were assigned to study the racial problem. (After examining the book sources) some of us students went to the Klan headquarters and the White Citizens' Councils. Then we said, 'What about the Montgomery Improvement Association?' To make a long

story short, we did go there and to the federal court hearings where Dr. King, Abernathy and Seay had been charged...In the process we met Dr. King and we asked them if it were possible for us to meet with some students from Alabama State. In the back of our minds this was in keeping with our assignment. By the time we met them the police got interested and they were following us: it became sort of an adventure thing. Eventually a nonviolent workshop was scheduled at the Baptist church. We asked Rev. Abernathy could we attend. 'Well,' he replied, 'if you come you will be arrested.' We said, 'Oh, we don't believe it. We have the right to come. We know the Constitution and everything.' He said, 'We want you to come, but we want you to know what's going to happen.'

By the end of the week (the police) knew who we all were and after the Saturday workshop the whole church was surrounded by police. There were five of us in the church—five white students—and the Rev. Abernathy told us the police informed him we would be arrested. (We decided to slip out the back door.) Sure enough we got back to the campus and after we were on campus about an hour the administration came and collected all of us and said, 'The police think you are still trapped in the church.' So we were asked to resign from the school on the grounds (that) what we were doing (was illegal).

Out of the five guys involved in that particular incident I was the only person out of the five that graduated. One attempted suicide. (The others) got tremendous pressure from their families. Mine was the only family that backed me up in the whole thing. In a sense they gave no white Southerner of that period any choice: you either capitulated absolutely and completely, or you became a rebel, a complete outlaw.[1]

Bob Zellner began working with SNCC as its representative on white college campuses, but was soon caught up in some of the most brutalizing campaigns staged by SNCC all over the South: Danville, Virginia; Baton Rouge, Louisiana; and McComb County, Mississippi. While protesting in the fall of 1961 in McComb County, he along with eight other SNCC staff members, were arrested and jailed. It happened this way: "He was the only white person in the long line walking toward the city hall....Men came out of the crowd, surrounded Zellner, and began clutching at him. (His two black SNCC associates) tried to shield him...Then the McComb police chief held Zellner while the men began to beat and to pull him into the crowd. He clutched at the railing, and tried to crawl up the steps. While the policemen watched, he was punched and kicked, his face scratched, his eyes gouged, and while on the ground he was kicked in the head repeatedly until he passed out. He regained consciousness in the police station, was pushed outside into an automobile, driven by the police chief fifteen miles, and let out."[2] They were found guilty in the court case that followed, and, unable to raise the $1,400 bail, they remained in jail for several months. Finally released, Bob and a friend immediately rode by bus to Baton Rouge where another SNCC worker was being held in jail. Being discouraged by the jailer in their efforts to visit the prisoner, their insistence got them arrested again, this time for vagrancy. The next morning they learned that their bail had been raised to the extravagant amount of $24,000, under the

[1] Clayborne Carson, ed., *Eyes on the Prize* (New York: Penguin Books, 1991) 127-9.
[2] Howard Zinn, *SNCC: The New Abolitionists* (Boston: Beacon Press, 1964) 171.

new charge of "criminal anarchy." Separated from his black associate, Bob lay awake all night, threatened with castration by the men in his cellblock. High school students were brought on tour of the Baton Rouge jail where they were told they could view "outside agitators." At Bob's cell the students were told, "Here's our white communist." After four weeks in jail, the two were formally arraigned, under the charge that they "...with force of arms feloniously did... advocate in public and in private opposition to the Government of the State of Louisiana by unlawful means and are members of the Student Nonviolent Coordinating Committee, an organization which is known to the offenders to advocate, teach and practice opposition to the State of Louisiana by unlawful means."[3]

Zellner, with his soft Southern personality, in fact conspicuously self-depreciating, had become the rare white who was allowed "to pitch" a freedom song at the protest rallies. He had actually devised one of his own to teach the black audiences. He recalled a hymn from Methodist camp meetings of his boyhood days in Alabama, a hymn entitled, "Been Down into the Sea." Two verses from his new freedom song run:

"I wanna go to heaven, but I wanna go right,
Been down into the South,
I don't wanna go without my civil rights,
Been down into the South.
"If you don't think I've been through hell,
Been down into the South,
Just follow me down to the Baton Rouge jail,
Been down into the South."

---

[3] Ibid., 174.

By the summer of 1963, Bob had accumulated some twenty-five arrests stemming from his movement activities in McComb, Baton Rouge, Montgomery, Albany, Georgia, and Talladega, Alabama. Still the Danville, Virginia, summer was yet ahead. For several weeks in 1963, Danville became another Birmingham. On the night of June 7, sixty-five black citizens—one lone white, Dorothy Miller—walked from the Bible Way Church to the city jail where previous demonstrators were lodged. The chief of police ordered them to stop singing. The minister instead passionately raised his voice in a loud prayer. The next moment he was led away by the police and fire hoses were turned on full force toward the remaining marchers. Police, including deputized city employees, clubbed those who dodged. Bob Zellner, photographing the episode, was arrested. Forty-eight demonstrators were treated at the city hospital. The force of the water had torn the dress off Gloria Campbell, the wife of the minister. The following day the Mayor declared, "We will hose down the demonstrators and fill every available stockade." During the successive days, the police violence worsened. One who was present has since written: "The city was under siege looking as if a police convention were in town, uniformed officers lingered in small groups on the streets or watched police cars gyrating around. State troopers patrolled in arrogant, slothful abundance. Fire trucks clanged and careened around the town. There were signs of a military mobilization taking place. I felt the city might blow apart."[4] Under such duress, Bob Zellner escaped Danville fearing for his life.

The ultimate indignity launched against Zellner was his arrest on the campus of Huntingdon College where he had finally managed to graduate. First charged with "conspiracy against the State of Alabama," it was reduced to "vagrancy." After two nights in the Montgomery jail, the state authorities contrived the more

---

[4] Ibid., 90.

serious criminal charge of "stealing a camera." Under this threat, they came to him with a compromise offer: "...if this boy would leave Montgomery and cause us no trouble in regard to race matters..." they would drop all charges. Zellner refused to cooperate and Charles Morgan, the civil rights attorney from Birmingham, agreed to take his case. Arguing for his client, Morgan declared that it was not the charge of felony which the prosecutors were pressing, rather it was because "my client is an integrationist, but when the day comes in this state that a man who disagrees can be charged and convicted of a crime, we will all be in trouble."[5] The jury could not reach a decision; it was declared a mistrial; and Bob Zellner was free.

---

[5] Charles Morgan, *A Time to Speak* (N.Y.: Harper and Row, 1964) 145.

SAM SHIRAH

On 23 April 1963, William Moore, a white Baltimore postman, marching to Mississippi with signs protesting racial discrimination, was murdered on an Alabama highway. Within a week, Sam Shirah, a twenty-year old white Alabamian, son of a Methodist minister, would join a select group of ten marchers who pledged to continue Moore's walk. On 23 April, SNCC had sent a wire to Alabama Governor George Wallace requesting protection for the walkers. He replied, "Your proposed actions, calculated to cause unrest, disorder, and a breach of the peace in the state of Alabama, will not be condoned or tolerated..."

When they departed Chattanooga on the first day of their march, Sam Shirah, in the lead, carried the signs Moore had worn, "Equal Rights for All (Mississippi or Bust)." The first night they spent on the floor of a Baptist church just over the line in Georgia. The second day they had trekked far enough to be near the Alabama line. They spent the second night dispersed in various black homes. So far, the state patrols and the national news people accompanied them with some degree of safety.

At a stop shortly before they reached the border, Sam Shirah wired Governor Wallace asking that he let the group pass through Alabama peacefully. Wallace had been a member of the church which Shirah's father had pastored, and had taught Sam in a Sunday school class when he was a boy. A diary kept by Bill

Hansen, another marcher, describes the scene as they reached the Alabama state line: "Planes were circling overhead. Down at the bottom of the hill and around a curve was a fence. Behind the fence over a thousand white people were massed, with Alabama policemen standing in front of them shoulder to shoulder. Traffic was stopped, and six or seven patrol cars stood alongside the road."[1] Alabama Public Safety Director Al Lingo was on hand to order the marchers to dispense. "Sam Shirah walked straight ahead, the rest following, and Lingo called for their arrest. The troopers rushed at them. Bob Zellner lay down and was dragged along the ground and into a police car. Eric Weinberger fell to the ground and the troopers used three-foot cattle prods on him, giving him repeated electric shocks, then four of them picked him up and threw him into a car."[2] Shirah and all the other nine were jailed on a charge of breaching the peace, then sent to Fort Kilbie, where they were kept on death row—in the same prison where the Scottsboro Boys were retained in 1931. After thirty-one days in jail, they were convicted of breach of peace and fined $200.

The authorities may have halted the "Freedom Walk," but not Shirah: just out of prison for little over a week, he joined Mary King on 19 June to work with the SNCC forces in Danville, Virginia. According to Mary's account, "We arrived at the High Street Baptist Church where Dorothy Miller would brief us on what had happened so far. We arrived at 8:00 A.M. on Saturday morning. Less than an hour later, I heard the Danville police, upstairs, kicking in the main door of the sanctuary of the church to arrest three SNCC workers who had been indicted by the grand jury...This was the first time I had been surrounded by police, state troopers, and deputized militia, and heard choppers in the

---

[1] Howard Zinn, *SNCC: The New Abolitionists* (Boston: Beacon Press, 1964) 178.

[2] Ibid., 179.

distance. I had never felt besieged before. I noticed a tightening nausea in my stomach. So this is what it is to be in dread. I thought, this is the sickening feeling of fear."[3] Shirah, Mary, Dorothy and some twelve other SNCC workers assigned to Danville were farmed out to various black families. Mary again:

> "These families, sometimes showing courage by taking us into their homes, gave us each a place to sleep, and they fed us physically and spiritually from whatever their own spare resources might be...The folks were warm, caring and inspiring. The local leadership wanted backup, support, and acknowledgment of the seriousness of its struggle. But we on the SNCC staff were certainly not necessary to fuel the fires raging in the hearts of Danville's black citizens, and we weren't the ones taking the major risks."[4]

Here, under such conditions, Shirah spent the three months of summer until he and all the SNCC workers were forced to flee the city to evade the grand jury indictment of "inciting to acts of violence and war."

---

[3] Mary King, *Freedom Song* (N.Y.: William Morrow Publishers, 1987) 90.
[4] Ibid., 91.

HENRY SCHWARZSCHILD

Henry Schwarzschild was an adopted Southerner; more properly, one should say, he had adopted the South. He had served in the military in the South (Ft. Benning, Georgia), married a girl from Kentucky, and had been naturalized an American citizen in the South. The obvious reason that this relationship was not mutual is because Schwarzchild identified with the blacks of the South, in addition to the fact that he was a Jew. Southerners tended to look down on Negroes and Jews, as if they were in the same inferior class. "In that period, in the heyday of the Movement, it was to a white man involved in the Civil Rights Movement in the South what was out there in the society was unremittingly hostile and dangerous. The only place you were welcome, at home, safe, loved and received, was in the black community, in whose bosom you lived and who loved you for being there."[1]

He had begun his witness for social justice for blacks rather inadvertently. While visiting his wife's home folks in Richmond, Kentucky, he and Kathy decided to drive over to Berea College, which Kathy had attended, to visit one of her old professors. He mentioned a protest to be held the next day against the segregated policies of the Main Street stores of Lexington, Kentucky. Since Kathy and he had already planned to pass through Lexington the

---

[1] Fred Powledge, *Free at Last* (Boston: Little, Brown and Company, 1991) 284.

next day, they precipitously decided to stop by. Since their baby was with them, Kathy decided to remain in the car. Henry recalls what happened then:

> I proceeded to join the demos outside the five-and-ten on the main drag of the town. We were not arrested. We only carried sandwich signs. The vivid memory I have is all the people from the countryside walking along the street and then stopping, amazed at this spectacle and lip reading our signs. We were certainly not in that sense technically a sit-in. Ours was more a sympathy demonstration with the sit-ins.[2]

But he was in for more serious trouble ahead. Since his family had escaped Germany ahead of the Holocaust, he, even though a little boy at the time, carried indelible memories of how the majority of Germans stood silently by while Jews were being persecuted.

> So the one thing that I concluded was that I would not want to say to myself at the end of my life that when there were enormously significant things going on in my society, I did nothing. The one unforgivable sin would be to stand by and let them happen and do nothing about them...It seemed to me that the Civil Rights Movement was (after the Hitler menace) the closest to that I would ever be.[3]

When he volunteered to ride with the SNCC Freedom Ride on the bus into Jackson, Mississippi, in 1961 he confessed to his fright: "I had the sense of the imminence of being killed under the open sky by somebody. And it was the first time in my life that I experienced that the old phrase about your knees knocking out of fear is

---

[2] Ibid., 239.
[3] Ibid., 237.

literally true. You are so tense that your muscles really shake, and my knees really did knock together. It was a very odd experience of terror."[4] As soon as the bus drove into the Jackson station, they were immediately arrested, taken to the paddy wagon and driven to the Hinds County jail. On 21 June 1961, Schwarzschild was sentenced "for the crime of breach of the peace" to four months in jail or a $200 fine. He stayed in jail a week and then paid his fine.

He has since described the feeling that descended on him as soon as the heavy doors clanged shut:

> It took me only a day or two to become all but numbed almost insensible by a kind of prison psychosis. I remember very well, somewhere in that week—and that's all it was for me—looking out through the window of that jail cell to the streets of Jackson, which were down below—we were up in the third or fourth floor—and seeing somebody, an ordinary person, walk down the street and at the corner, cross the street and turn left and go on the next side street. And I remember the sense of utter strangeness; of disbelief that one could, in this world about whose reality I seemed to remember nothing, turn left and go down the street if one wanted to turn left and go down the street, in a few days it had sort of evaporated as a reality. I was utterly numbed by the terror of being in here. One didn't know what would happen to one; you didn't know whether you could get out.[5]

That is how Schwarzschild described years later his feelings at the time.

---

[4] Ibid., 284.
[5] Ibid., 285.

JANE STEMBRIDGE

Jane Stembridge, a Baptist preacher's daughter who had grown up in Georgia but was momentarily enrolled at Union Theological School in New York city, immediately responded to the sit-ins when they commenced in Greensboro, North Carolina. She drove down to Raleigh for the Easter weekend (1960) conference which was the beginning of the Student Nonviolent Coordinating Committee. She describes her reaction as a white Southerner:

> The most inspiring moment for me was the first time I heard the students sing 'We Shall Overcome.'...There was no SNCC, no ad hoc committees, no funds, just people who did not know what to expect but who came and released the common vision in that song. I had just driven down from Union Seminary—out of it, except that I cared, and that I was a Southerner...It was inspiring because it was the beginning, and because, in a sense, it was the purest moment. I am a romantic. But I call this moment the one...[1]

From that tenuous contact, she was phoned back at her studies in New York and given the job as SNCC's first office secretary when it set up in cramped quarters in Atlanta in June. She was

---

[1] Howard Zinn, *SNCC: The New Abolitionists* (Boston: Beacon Press, 1964) 33.

employed by a loosely knit organization of delegates from sixteen Southern states, but the action was taking place in the "hi-ways and by-ways." The central office had the almost impossible task of getting the many spontaneous upstarts to adhere to their initial Statement of Purpose: "We affirm the philosophical or religious ideal of non-violence as the foundation of our purpose, the pre-supposition of our faith, and the manner of our action..."[2] Jane was exposed to the real action when she joined one of the Atlanta lunch-counter sit-ins where hundreds of students were engaged:

> ...the most honest moment—the one in which I saw the gutstype truth—stripped of anything but total fear and total courage: Lana Taylor from Spelman was sitting next to me. The manager walked up behind her, said something obscene, and grabbed her by the shoulders. 'Get the hell out of here, nigger.' Lana was not going. I do not know whether she should have collapsed in nonviolent manner. She probably did not know. She put her hands under the counter and held. He was rough and strong. She just held and I looked down at the moment at her hands...brown, strained...every muscle holding...All of a sudden he let go and left. I thought he knew he could not move that girl—ever.[3]

Jane reflected on her experiences with SNCC by writing poetry and meditative pieces. This one describes how she viewed SNCC: "...finally it all boils down to human relationships. It has nothing to do finally with governments. It is the question of whether we...whether I shall go on living in isolation or whether there shall be a we. The student movement is not a cause...it is a collision between this one person and that one person. I am going to sit beside you...Love alone is radical. Political statements are not;

---

[2] Ibid., 34.
[3] Ibid., 39.

programs are not; even going to jail is not."[4] For five years, she moved toward and away from SNCC, never far from it but sometimes withdrawing for a period. Her tour of duty in the Mississippi Delta brought her almost to despair. "It reminds you of people beginning to be colder than before. The sky is very blue and smoke is coming out of the chimneys, out of kitchens. We do need food and clothes so bad...There won't be enough food, nor enough warmth for this winter as there wasn't for last, nor for the one before that."[5] "Poverty negates the strength of being poor," Jane decided. In the face of the growing militarization of the state of Mississippi in 1963 and 64, to combat the civil rights workers, Jane reflected: "...(There) is nothing ultimate about the Mississippi legislature, although it seems so at times, realizing that they will never be able to issue an injunction against April nor legislate a leaf...On the other side of the wall people are getting ready too—their riot helmets, their baby-blue tanks, their shotguns and motorcycles are for real and their horrible hate and fear. So we're over here on our side of town and they're over there on theirs and nobody can cross the line. We are two sides and we never can speak together or even cry."[6] When Jim Chaney, Andy Goodman and Mickey Schwermer were murdered in Mississippi in June 1964, Jane wrote an Open Letter to America that concluded: "We are in Mississippi this morning because we believed what we learned in the schools of this country—freedom and justice for all—but we did not see freedom and justice. We are here because we believe in this nation...We are your children, living what you taught us as Truth."[7] Her plaintive plea did not stop the authorities. Under a temporary injunction issued in the capitol,

---

[4] Ibid., 7.
[5] Mary King, *Freedom Song* (N.Y.: William Morrow Publishers, 1987) 135.
[6] Ibid., 327.
[7] Ibid., 397.

Jackson, all civil rights groups were made illegal. Jane Stembridge was arrested in Greenwood and held under $1,000 bail.

As SNCC proceeded on its inevitable bureaucratic route, and as self-appointed black leaders managed to dominate under the slogan "Black Power," Jane felt herself being eased out. She who had been the first executive secretary of the struggling pioneer group now felt that SNCC was losing its vision. She feared that it was paying more attention to procedures, operations, gadgetry—what she called "apparatus"—than to its early radical concepts of nonviolence and its regard for persons. So she wrote a poem:

> where
> in all
> the awful
> apparatus
> we acquired
> to hasten
> freedom
> is
> the flute
> which
> thinner
> than
> the
> rain
> rings
> freedom
> in[8]

---

[8] Ibid., 440.

ROBERT GRAETZ AND GLENN SMILEY

During the year long Montgomery bus boycott of 1956, Martin
Luther King Jr. concluded in his book, *Stride Toward Freedom*,
"Not a single white group would take the responsibility of
preparing the white community. We tried to get the white
ministerial alliance to make a simple statement calling for courtesy
and Christian brotherhood...but Robert Graetz reported that the
majority 'dared not get involved in such a controversial issue.'"[1]
The exception was the Reverend Robert Graetz, the white pastor of
the black Trinity Lutheran Church in Montgomery. He worked
closely with King in both the Council on Human Relations and as
an Executive Board member of the Montgomery Improvement
Association, and later on as its secretary. Therefore, it could be
expected that he would be the target of white extremist terrorism.
The prevailing white attitude was that the black population was
contented and any unrest manifest by them had to have been
instigated by some "superior" white person. Graetz, who was born
in West Virginia and had spent his ministry in the South,
subsequently received the brunt of white hostility. In early January,
1956, Graetz's home was bombed as well as the home of Dr. King.
Later his home was bombed a second time. The Reverend Graetz

---

[1] Martin Luther King Jr., *Stride Toward Freedom* (N.Y.: Harper and Brothers,
1958) 169.

planted a tree in the bomb crater on his front lawn and reminded those who came to its dedication that "while in the midst of life there is death, so in the midst of death there is life." He paid dearly for all his activity in support of the boycott. Apart from almost nightly telephone threats and broken windows, the police jailed and threatened him for helping in the carpool. Graetz did not back down and when the federal order to desegregate the buses reached Montgomery on 13 November of that year he had his moment of glory at the mass rally on Wednesday night, the 14th. Eight thousand people crowded the two churches where the celebration took place. Graetz on the platform with King and Dr. Ralph Abernathy read the scripture, using Paul's famous letter from 1 Corinthians 13. When he reached the part that reads "but when I became a man I put away childish things," the congregation burst into applause, shouting and cheering and waving their handkerchiefs as if to say they knew they had come of age.

The other white Southerner that played a significant role in the Montgomery boycott was Glenn Smiley. He had grown up on a cotton farm in Texas, and in spite of studying religion while in college and being ordained a minister in the Southern Methodist Conference, he remained true to the segregated pattern of his culture. By the time the United States entered the Second World War, he had become affiliated with the pacifist organization, the Fellowship of Reconciliation, and, accordingly, refused to honor his draft classification as a conscientious objector. Thus he was placed in a federal penitentiary for his defiance, and there he saw first hand the results of racial separation within the walls of the prison. While in prison, the FOR itself was moving from mere anti-militarism to anti-racist action. Its leaders formed an offshoot that took the name Congress of Racial Equality. Smiley, released from prison in 1945, helped establish a CORE chapter in Los Angeles. King asked Bayard Rustin, a leader in both FOR and

CORE, if he knew someone who could supervise the day-to-day training in non-violence during the bus boycott in Montgomery. On 14 February 1956, Smiley joined King for this general assignment. King spelled out four definite needs:

> He wanted me (1) to teach him all the Gandhian non-violence that I knew; (2) to serve as an informal but open source of intelligence in the white community; (3) to teach people in Montgomery all I knew about Gandhian nonviolence; (4) to go throughout the South and build support groups and see if we couldn't make a movement out of this.[2]

What it boiled down to practically was, as Smiley later recalled, basically two assignments: "One was at every mass meeting I was given a spot on the program to discuss tactical nonviolence. Then, I was supposed to go around to the different churches and meet with small groups and try to whip the clergy and laity into line about nonviolence. My other assignment was to make every contact possible in the white community and attempt to do the same thing, to get them to understand and try to meet the Negroes."[3] Smiley wrote the guide-sheet in preparation for the blacks of Montgomery boarding the city buses for the first time after their victorious legal battle; the day set was 21 December 1956. Called "Suggestions for Integrating Buses," it was mimeographed and distributed throughout the city. Listed among its many guidelines were such as these: No. 2. "The whole bus is now for the use of all people. Take any vacant seat." No. 6. "Remember this is not a victory for Negroes alone, but for all Montgomery and the South. Do not boast! Do not brag!" No. 8.

---

[2] Richard Deats, "Glenn Smiley, The Gentle Persuader," *Fellowship Magazine,* (November/December) 1993: 15.
[3] David Chappell, *Inside Agitators* (Baltimore: Johns Hopkins University Press, 1994) 60.

"Be loving enough to absorb evil and understanding enough to turn an enemy into a friend."

While Smiley was strengthening the blacks, the Montgomery City Commissioners were preparing to stonewall. On December 18, they issued this document:

> The City Commission, and we know our people are with us in this determination, will not yield one inch, but will do all in its power to oppose the integration of the Negro race with the white race in Montgomery, and will forever stand like a rock against social equality, intermarriage, and mixing of the races under God's creation and plan.[4]

Smiley, for his part, assembled about ninety white people in a church who prepared themselves for the equal sitting on the buses the next day, training them in the same methods of non-violence and mutual acceptance. As for himself, he approached King with the request that he might sit beside King as they took the first integrated bus ride in the city. The photograph of the two seated side by side went around the world, and King included it in his first book, *Stride Toward Freedom*.

Later, with King organizing the Southern Christian Leadership Conference, Smiley was called in to calm down conflicts within its ranks. By 1968, he was an advance preparer in Washington, D.C., making plans for the Poor People's Campaign. Holding a workshop in a black church, instructing about two hundred team leaders on how to conduct themselves peacefully in their marches around the city, Smiley learned of King's assassination in

---

[4] King, *Stride Toward Freedom*, 197.

Memphis. He spent much of the rest of his life establishing Martin Luther King centers for nonviolence in places all over the world.

ROBERT BROWN

One night in June 1969, the Trinity Baptist Church of Lexington, Kentucky, went up in flames. White supremacists had set fire to the church and it burned to the ground before firefighters could squelch the flames. Dr. Robert Brown, its pastor, watched the tragedy: "As I stood that June morning and watched the church burn to the ground, I remember I literally sobbed in the arms of Dr. Homer Nutter....He held me like a father. And I understood that he had suffered too."[1] Dr. Nutter was black, Dr. Brown was white. They had hitherto cemented their relationship in the city of Lexington, where they both pastored, because of their civil rights concern. Exactly eight years before the burning, the Trinity Church had voted to integrate. That had caused a split in its membership, had left its pastor isolated among his Baptist ministerial colleagues, and had created lasting resentment among the die-hard white segregationists of the city. This night was payback time.

Brown had become pastor of Trinity in 1958 and within three years its congregation had grown from 200 to 600. The church had developed an active ministry to the handicapped and the retarded, and had erected a new building. Everything was on up-and-up,

---

[1] All the facts and quotations in this chapter are taken from Carolyn Dupont's unpublished paper read at the Blue Grass Symposium, at the University of Kentucky, March 1999.

until... Until the deaf group regularly attending the First Baptist Church which provided simultaneous sign language was rejected by that congregation because it had inducted an African-American who was deaf. Three other Baptist churches that were invited to accept the integrated group also refused. So the group approached Brown and Trinity Church. The Deacon Board was apprehensive, but Brown believing it was the right thing to do brought it before the entire congregation. Nearly five hundred members came to its business meeting that lasted for more than three hours. Brown reported,

> Everything was said at that meeting that has ever been said about integration, racial differences, inner-racial marriage, loving your neighbor, etc. It was a tense, emotional meeting. Most of us realized that when it was over our church would never be the same. We voted 431 for integration and only 27 against. Everyone was shocked at the vote. I knew who the 27 were though, and I was apprehensive. Eventually 23 of the 27 would leave the church.

The twenty-three who left were key leaders and major financial contributors, and the church immediately plunged into deep financial crisis. Brown persisted though, in spite of bad health apparently resulting from the hostile pressures, and increased his participation in the city's efforts to integrate. Still he felt completely alone among Lexington's white clergy. His closest friends became the Black ministers with whom he now shared his inmost concerns. Ironically, he dubbed himself "Lexington's Lone White Freedom Rider."

Nonetheless, at the time of the burning, Trinity was still predominantly white and Brown longed for more than "token" integration. They decided to use the devastation to initiate a greater campaign of bridging the gap between the races in the city.

Their launching of a bus ministry into the inner city changed the racial composition of Trinity within sixty days. This time a few more whites left, but over the years Trinity has established the reputation as one of the truly "integrated Southern Baptist churches." And Brown finally felt satisfied with the relative achievement of his goals. "I have in every true sense been a Pastor to black people....It has been a comfortable experience for me." From the ashes of white-citizenry-hate there had arisen a phoenix of immortal hope.

J. W. WARING

When desegregation was ordered by the Supreme Court decision of 1954, the public servants most likely to be effected were the police, the schoolteachers, and the judges. They were on the front line of radical change: ardently resisted by most whites and eagerly awaited by the blacks. Moreover, under the prevailing mores of Southern white racism, they were obliged to enforce, sometimes with over-zealous harshness, the organized resistance to accepting integration. Thus, unwittingly and sometimes unwillingly—they became the public bulwarks of bitter white defense. Therefore the few federal judges—nearly all appointed by conservative political power—who ruled in favor of obeying the Brown decision were immediately unpopular and subject to scurrilous personal attacks. Judge Frank Johnson of Alabama, Judge James McMillan of North Carolina, and Judge J. W. Waring of South Carolina are outstanding examples of the few who bore the brunt of this public reaction. Faced with the dilemma of supporting the Southern way of life in which they were reared and which had raised them to their privileged post of upholding the Constitution of the United States to which they were sworn, they reacted both conscientiously and professionally. And they paid a price.

Judge J. W. Waring of Charleston was hit the hardest. Because of the two major decisions, his court made on desegregation; one was the Clarendon County case, known as *Briggs v. Elliott*, which was one of the five cases to reach the Warren-led US Supreme Court and eventuated as the *Brown v. Board of Education* decision of 1954. When he was appointed a federal district judge in 1942, at the age of sixty-one, he had earned that political plumb for having been a model Southerner. Born in Charleston of the best of the city's families, educated there and practicing law there, he had all the right connections. No one could have foreseen that this judge would ultimately make two of the most innovative judicial rulings in favor of integration, one on 12 July 1947, the other on 23 June 1951. But from the time of his appointment to the moment of those decisions, he had made some radical changes in his life. First, he had divorced and remarried—this time to a woman who had was sensitive to racial inequities. Second, in his reading, both in racial matters and judicial correctness, he was opening his mind. Over those early years, he made a few minor changes in his court: desegregation of the seating and jury roster, mandatory use of courtesy titles, and the hiring of a black bailiff. But it was his July 1947 decision—giving blacks equal voting rights in South Carolina—when he finally broke with his racist colleagues. "Negroes are voting in Texas and even in Georgia. I cannot see where the skies will fall if South Carolina is put in the same class with these and other states....It is time for South Carolina to rejoin the Union."[1] On the same day, he ruled that the University of South Carolina law school must admit a black applicant. Statewide public wrath descended upon him. He was now a pariah in all the associations which had here-to-fore accepted him gladly: his clubs, his church, his neighborhood, the state Democratic Party. Even his nephew, who managed the editorial page of the Charleston News & Courier, denounced him. He was now without honor in his hometown.

---

[1] David Chappell, *Inside Agitators* (Baltimore: Johns Hopkins University Press, 1994) 409.

But that reaction paled besides the south-wide reaction to his dissenting opinion in the three-judge federal court decision of June 23, 1951. This dealt with the famous Clarendon County suit filed by Thurgood Marshall to integrate the public schools. Known as the Briggs vs. Elliott case, it was the first of five suits across the nation that, in unison, reached the U.S. Supreme Court as *Brown v. Board of Education.* Judge Waring, when first approached by the NAACP lawyers, maneuvered to get the case heard in his court—the other two judges obliged to come, one from North Carolina, the other from upstate South Carolina. Apparently he foresaw the significance of this case for American history and wanted it heard first in Charleston. When the day came, and the long file of black parties to the litigation filled the courtroom, Judge Waring viewed it "as if they had come there on a pilgrimage." The conclusion of the hearing, however, was a foregone verdict; the other two federal judges were die-hard segregationists. Judge Waring's dissent has since been described as "his swan song from the court." He told a reporter from Ohio, "I've got a cause to live for and a job to do. What can they do to me, at seventy-one, that would matter?"[2] He declared in his lone dissent that the only question before the court was the doctrine of segregation. The Fourteenth Amendment was intended to guarantee minorities their full rights as citizens. Segregation, he held, is as harmful to white as to black children. "Segregation in education can not be equal...Segregation is per se inequality."

History may well mark that moment, in legal proceedings, as the first and clearest enunciation of the end of segregation in America. It would take decades for the higher courts, the education systems across the nation and the public in general to reach Judge Waring's pronouncement on that day. Three years later, 17 May 1954, Chief Justice Earl Warren, reading the unanimously

---

[2] Ibid., 596.

approved Brown decision, would use a rephrasing of Judge Waring's: "Separate educational facilities are inherently unequal." Judge Waring was also aware that he had preached his own doom in the city of his birth and in the South. South Carolina was in shock, as well as much of the South. For Waring was speaking three years before the hated "Earl Warren Court," and, more importantly, he was speaking, not as a despised outsider, but as a native son. They couldn't believe their ears. He was completely abandoned now and was obliged to depart the region. Within six months, he retired from the bench and he and his wife moved to New York City where they lived until his death in 1968. His sole return to Charleston was to be in his coffin. Fewer than a dozen whites joined the throng of black mourners at his funeral.

PAUL TURNER

In December 1956, Clinton, Tennessee, was known worldwide as the little town in the South ruled by a mob of white racists opposed to school integration. Earlier Governor Frank Clement was forced to use the National Guard to quell mob violence and to restore civil order. The white racist agitators, led by the out-of-state segregationist, John Kasper, then shifted tactics and fielded a slate of White Citizens' Council candidates for the city council and for mayor to be voted on election day, Tuesday, 5 December. In September, only twelve Negro students had enrolled in the previously all-white Clinton High School. But the massive and continuous violence against them had forced them to decide to stay home until they had some assurance that they would be protected. The principal could do nothing; in fact, he himself and his wife were also targets—eventually forced to resign and leave the town. He confessed on the CBS television documentary produced by Edward R. Murrow in January 1957, "Someone threatened to throw acid in my face, said I wasn't fit to live. My wife and I are always careful going home; we study the premises first, lock the doors, investigate every noise. It's just a constant thing to wear myself and my wife down."[1]

---

[1] Quoted in Margaret Anderson, *The Children of the South* (New York: Farrar, Straus and Giroux, 1966) 21.

On election day morning, Dr. Paul Turner, pastor of the First Baptist Church (white), decided to do something about this shameful display of undemocratic—and to his mind, unchristian—behavior. He, along with two other white leaders of the town, went to the homes of the Black students and offered to escort them to school. They were jeered and heckled as they passed through the mob usually gathered to prevent the Blacks from attending. All the way down the long hill leading from the residential area to the school Pastor Turner kept repeating to the children, "Don't be afraid, no one is going to hurt you, don't be afraid."

More than a score of ruffians followed Turner as he left school. As he reached the middle of the street opposite the courthouse, about two blocks away, they assaulted him. He was beaten about the face and on the head, but the police intervened just in time to prevent him from being killed. His wife explained in the aftermath: "Paul felt the time had come to do something on this—and I know he had thought about it very carefully and believed in it thoroughly. He felt it was his responsibility. We've had this tension too long."[2]

The so-called "silent, good people" of the town were shocked. They could not believe this sort of act could happen in their midst. As a result, the White Citizens' Council slate was defeated by a large majority. Sixteen persons were arrested for violating a permanent injunction. The Black children were assured that henceforth city police and sheriff's deputies would protect them daily from violence and threats. The act of violence against Pastor Turner seemed to bring the town to its senses as nothing else could have. The editor of the town paper, who had previously defended segregation, said, "The attack on Paul Turner solidified the feeling of the community, bringing us to the point where we stood up and

---

[2] Quoted in *Interracial News Service* (Vol. 29, May-June, 1958, Number 3).

said we believe in law and order."³ A white fellow-student declared, "I thought I didn't want the Negroes here. Now I don't know. I couldn't want to be like those people who beat up the preacher."⁴ One of the twelve, a Black named Bobby Cain, graduated that year, the first African-American to be graduated from a state-supported high school in Tennessee.

The following Sunday morning, the Rev. Dr. Paul Turner was back in his pulpit, his face still swollen. He faced a full house on the theme, "There is no color line at the cross." He minced no words: "When mobs brought chaos to our town in September, I talked with a 'radio preacher' from Georgia. He had come here to join in the fight against desegregation. As an apostle of the 'Curse of Canaan' doctrine, he believed an eternal curse rested upon all Negroes....There is no reasonable (much less Biblical) basis to prove that the Negro race is cursed, or is inherently inferior....As one of our citizens put it this week: 'If we are not against integration, and if we're not against segregation, we surely are against disintegration.'...Truth and love are sterile concepts unless they are incarnated in life actions and attitudes...As I know my own motivations, this is how I see my involvement in the problems of our community. That by identifying with those in need I have preached a sermon to my world about Christ far beyond any homiletical masterpiece I may deliver to you in words."⁵

³ Anderson, *The Children of the South*, 19.
⁴ Ibid., 19.
⁵ Wayne Dahoney, ed., *Baptists See Black* (Waco, Texas: Word Book, 1969) 12-16.

IRA HARKEY

For four months in 1962-63, Pascagoula, Mississippi was virtually under siege by an organized gang of white supremacists. It maintained quasi-legal status by virtue of the fact that its leader was the Jackson County sheriff. The gang had gained local fame by driving to Oxford to join the campus melee following the entrance of James Meredith to the University on 30 September 1962. Led by the sheriff, a caravan of cars and a chartered bus carried the gang to Oxford where they joined in the rock throwing and property destruction in spite of the presence of US Marshalls. They boasted back in Pascagoula that none had outdone them in brick throwing and vehicle burning. Encouraged by their enthusiastic reception by the local citizenry, they decided to organize permanently, going so far as to secure a charter and calling themselves "Jackson County Citizens Emergency Unit." Their program of "civic improvement" was to eradicate local "nigger-lovers," to boycott all businesses that employed or sold goods to Negroes, to "attend to" any persons put on their suspect list, to train a strong-arm squad to accomplish these purposes, and, above all, to put out of business Pascugoula's daily paper, *The Chronicle*, identified by them as "the leading nigger-lover in the state."

The editor of *The Chronicle*, Ira Harkey, was a native Mississippian, forty-four years old. He had taken over the paper in 1949 after mustering out of the Navy as a Lieutenant, and would operate it for fourteen years until he was forced from the County. He knew well the 600-member Jackson County Emergency Unit. As he tells it,

> For four months—from October 1962 to February, 1963—my newspaper was the target of a campaign of vilification, boycott, threats and actual violence. A rifle slug was fired through my front door and a shotgun shell blasted out the windows in my office. Hate spewed into the Chronicle telephones and mail box, grown men grabbed and shook and cursed our carrier boys on the street, advertisers were threatened and dropped their space, the high sheriff himself chased a Negro carrier boy off his route....so thoroughly did the poison of hate permeate upward from the gutter that a lady librarian....wrote me that 'instead of a bullet through your door I hope you get a bullet through your stupid head."[1]

Earlier, the Ku Klux Klan had initiated the overt persecution by burning crosses in select places around the town. On 1 September 1955, a few days before the opening of the school year crosses were burned before the Negro school, the largest Negro church, and in front of the home of editor Harkey.

> One of my startled children first saw the blaze in front of our house and ran screaming to his mother. White-faced, round-eyed, she called me. I went out and hosed the evil thing. A message had been left, painted on a piece of brown corrugated cardboard. 'We do not appreciate niggerlovers. We are watching you. KKK.'...No one not rooted in the South can understand the full terror of a cross burning, this classic threat from the Klan. It is like the voice of doom, the sentence of death, the placing of the victim beyond the pale. Marking him for punishment by some of

[1] Ira Harkey, *The Smell of Burning Crosses* (Jacksonville, Ill.: Harris-Wolfe and Co.) 14.

the most ruthless thugs in the history of mankind. I did not let my wife and children see how profoundly I was shaken. I grinned, an idiot expression I was to try to wear through the next nine years of violence and threats and in my column the next week I hailed the year's new season with, 'Ah, autumn! Falling leaves...the hint of a north breeze stirring in the night...the smell of burning crosses in the air.'[2]

The Chronicle took a financial beating over the years from its loss of advertisers and subscribers due to its editor's opinions, especially those pertaining to his periodic endorsement of integration and his attacks on the state politicians who led the resistance to integration and the promotion of hate and prejudice against the black citizens of Mississippi. Nonetheless, Harkey believed he could hold out. In one editorial, he opined: "We do know beyond doubt, however, that just as spite and hate will never build a going concern, spite and hate will not sink an enterprise that is honestly run and supplies a genuine need."[3] However, as time went on, he had less and less local support. In the end, he had to admit: "In Pascagoula, there was no power to which I could turn for help." Not the County Board of Supervisors, not the Mayor, not the Chamber of Commerce; not even the ministers of the local churches. "Three members of the Ministerial Union of Protestant churchmen came to visit me, the torment of their souls visible in their eyes," but they made it clear they would not take up his cause. In the first editorial he ever positioned on page one, he tried to emphasize to the Pascagoulans that this was not Harkey's fight alone but theirs as well. Titled "You May Be Next," it ended with the words, "We are under no illusions that anybody here cares what happens to Ira Harkey. But think long on this: what happens to him can happen to you. You may be next." In the end,

---

[2] Ibid., 104.
[3] Ibid., 164.

he lost. "I found I could not remain in Pascagoula, could not bear to exist in the vacuum of an ostracism that remained in force even after victory (he had defeated the JCCEU), could not function in a silence of total isolation as if I were underwater or in galactic space. I was a pariah." He sold *The Chronicle* and moved his family from the town. "I was told later that as I walked from *The Chronicle* office for the last time, a reporter I had recently hired from upstate wrung his hands and drooled, 'Boy, I can't wait to start writing nigger again!'"[4]

How did Ira Harkey, a native Mississippian raised in the same atmosphere of cultural prejudice, become an exception and champion the case of universal brotherhood? In trying to explain this himself, he tells that even as a youth he had misgivings:

"...because I believed what I was first taught in Sunday school even though it became apparent soon enough that grown up whites did not and did not expect anyone else really to believe it applied to any but white people; because I believed also in the rightness of what I was first taught in school about democracy; because I read much and identified with and thrilled to the eventual triumph of the underdog in history and literature...But most of all, I got this way because of one moment in the western Pacific in 1945 when all these thoughts and feelings I had lived with for nearly twenty years came together in my mind on the flight deck of a crippled aircraft carrier."

On 22 January 1945, a returning plane hit the deck and its remaining bombs exploded on impact. Fifty-two of his fellows were dead and hundreds wounded. The next day, while participating in their funeral, he soberly watched the canvas bags containing the bodies of the fifty-two slide over the deck into the ocean waters, one by one. "As I watched the blue canvas sacks slip

---

[4] Ibid., 15, 17, 18, 19.

over the side the conviction came to me that the Negro, who is good enough to be gutted by an unsegregated explosion, to be trussed in an unsegregated sack, to be dumped into an unsegregated ocean and dispatched to an unsegregated heaven or hell, is just exactly good enough to live an unsegregated life in the nation of his birth. And I thought further that the Southern Negro, in his century of unemancipated emancipation, has shown himself through his infinite patience and incredible loyalty to be the best American that there is. And I am grateful to him. And I still do. I have an inexpressible feeling about the value of the Negro as a symbol of Americanism and about the lesson in patriotism his wretched life can teach all others of us less qualified to call ourselves Americans."[5]

---

[5] Ibid., 207.

DUNCAN GRAY

When the rioting raged that Sunday evening, 30 September 1962, on the University of Mississippi campus, there were two forces pitted against each other. Besides the university students protesting James Meredith's (the first black applicant accepted at the University) coming to the campus accompanied by federal marshals, there were hundreds of citizens from all over the state who rallied to the side of Governor Ross Barnett and his adamant resistance to integration. Radio and television stations across the state had run repeated invitations for all to come. Speeches by General Edwin Walker, the Texan who had resigned from the military to take up arms against the "integrationists," were broadcast for days prior. "Ten thousand strong...Bring your flags, your tents, and your skillets. It is time. Now or never." They came with weapons—machine guns, rifles, dynamite and swords. Pascagoula, far down on the Gulf coast, for instance, sent a caravan of cars and a chartered bus, all armed and eager for a fight. The local law enforcement units as well as the State Highway Patrol, which were both around the campus when the marshals arrived, stood idly by while the killing and the destruction mounted, or they simply drove out of town. Twenty-nine U.S. Marshals were shot that night, and 160 other marshals were wounded by bricks, pipes, bottles and lumber hurled at them. One rioter commandeered a bulldozer from a campus construction site and drove it recklessly toward the line of marshals until it miraculously careened out of control. General Walker positioned himself in the center of the rioters, to be their leader and spokesman.

The other force that night was a single voice of calm and reason, the rector of the local St. Peter's Episcopal Church. The Reverend Duncan Gray, thirty-six years old, forced himself through the violent throng and sidled up to the Confederate Soldiers Monument to join General Walker. When he tried to speak, the mob yelled, "Kill him! Kill him!" This time, they meant not Meredith, but the minister. "Traitor! Traitor! Let me at the goddammed scalawag!" "Please, please, I beg of you; don't do this. Please return to your homes..."—before he could finish he was jerked from the pedestal and flung into the crowd. He and a fellow priest were struck repeatedly until the campus police intervened. His brave but ineffectual effort did not salvage the night; it was the sudden appearance of a unit of the local National Guard, commanded by one of his own parishioners, Captain Murray Faulkner, nephew of the novelist, William Faulkner. But the rector's words that night and his continued presence throughout the evening, working for peace, carried considerable weight. His father, Bishop of the Mississippi diocese, was also a member of the University's Board of Trustees. And Duncan Gray, Jr. was well known throughout the state, and even the nation, for having spent his career openly fighting racism. By no means could he be labeled a "scalawag" since he was born in Mississippi and four generations of his family had now served at one time or another the parish of St. Peter's. That fact, more than anything else, explains the vehement reaction of the mob to his appeal. A white Mississippi preacher who openly and aggressively advocated integration of the races in 1962 was intolerable.

Duncan had begun his crusade early in life. While attending the theology school at the University of the South at Sewanee,

Tennessee, the authorities had reaffirmed the school's lily-white tradition. Eight professors issued an ultimatum that they would resign at the end of that school year, 1953, if the seminary did not open its doors to blacks. Duncan at the time was on a student mission assignment in Cuba, but on his return to the campus in the fall of 1953, he was elected president of the seminary's student-body. He immediately engineered a motion supporting the eight signators: "Resolved...that this society expresses hereby its full confidence in the professional competence and integrity of each member of the faculty..."[1]

He pushed this move in spite of the fact that his own uncle was the President of Sewanee and would be the one to force the eight faculty members to resign. His senior paper ended with a plea that the Episcopal Church lead the way by the abolition of every appearance of segregation within its own body. He knew he was taking on an empire of resistance, including that of his own father, the Bishop. He was now becoming his church's thorn-in-the-flesh, and was soon to be "the most hated man in the state."

This last opprobrium he earned by writing the official document of the diocese called "The Church Considers the Supreme Court Decision," 1 July 1954. Although the youngest member on the Diocese's Department of Christian Social Relations—also the youngest cleric in the diocese and having been ordained only eight months—, he composed the final draft, twelve pages. It was published in the diocesan paper and later produced in a pamphlet (no state printer wanted his name on the publication). For most Christians in the state, its message of gracefully accepting and implementing the Supreme Court's mandate to desegregate was blasphemous and heretical. Within the diocese, parish after parish acted to disown it. A state senator wrote Gray: "I shall do

[1] Will Campbell, *And Also With You—Duncan Gray and the American Dilemma* (Franklin, Tennessee: Providence House Publishers, 1997) 83.

everything humanly possible to insure permanent segregation in public schools...I do not see how anyone could consider this decision other than as one rendered by a stacked court at the behest of the NAACP and other allied organizations, most of which are treasonable and subversive."[2] There were hundreds of letters, some polite and well-meaning demurrers. Far more were threats, insults, diatribes of vitriol and vituperation, all designed to frighten the Delta priest back into the chancel of silence.

These successions of little blows became the winds to strengthen his sinews for that night on the Confederate Monument along side General Walker. The two represented both sides of the South, but Duncan Gray Jr. measured up to those few Southern whites who Martin Luther King Jr. felt contributed to his dream of the beloved community.

---

[2] Ibid., 139.

SARAH BOYLE

Sarah Patton Boyle was a middle-aged housewife, mother of two and married to a college professor, when her life was turned up side down by her stand on integration. Little had distinguished her career from the other white Virginia women privileged to belong to the "blue blood" of the state. Her father had been an honored Episcopal clergyman, and she had moved in the highest circle of society enjoying the benefits of segregation. Residing in Charlottesville, where the University of Virginia was located, she considered herself and all her friends to be liberal, quite proud that any concerns she manifested toward the Negroes in town was of the noblesse-oblige variety.

She got her chance to expose her "maternalism" (as she later had the courage to label it) in 1950, when Gregory Swanson was the first black to be accepted in the University, as a student in the law school. She immediately got in touch with him; first, by writing effusive letters of welcome, then, by trying to assist him in locating a room—of course, in the Negro part of town. Then, she conceived the bright idea of publishing an article about his entrance into Thomas Jefferson's institution—how nice it was that at last the liberalism of the place had won out. It would be entitled, "We Want a Negro at UVA," and she envisioned it being published in *Reader's Digest*. When she finally confronted Swanson with a draft of the article, he dampened her enthusiasm by bluntly requesting her not to publish it. "I just want to be a student like any other." About the same time, she published a letter in the state's leading newspaper, the *Richmond Times-Dispatch*, answering an article demanding that the state close down any institution ordered by the Supreme Court to admit Negroes.

> I was keenly conscious of having laid my neck on the railroad track as I mailed this missive. To publish such a letter in one of the South's most widely circulated newspapers was to lift a voice as loudly as it could be lifted in Virginia. To my knowledge, this was the first time a white Virginian had spoken above a whisper in support of integration at the University. Even my most liberal friends doubtless would disapprove.[1]

In spite of her high hopes, rooted in her belief that informed liberalism would win the day, she received not a single letter of commendation for her efforts, either from the whites of the extended University family or from the blacks. Not a word of support, not a word of attack. There-upon she submitted it to the editor of the local Negro paper, T. J. Sellers, for his frank opinion. His conclusion hit the heart of her problem: "There is a New Negro in our midst who is insisting that America wake up and recognize the fact that he is a man like other men. He is entirely out of sympathy with the gross paternalism of the 'Master class' turned liberal."[2] And what was Mrs. Boyle's reaction? "I have known no experience more distressing than the discovery that Negroes didn't love me. Unutterable loneliness claimed me. I felt without roots; like a man without a country."[3] Her developing friendship with the black editor saved her. As she put it, she

---

[1] Sarah Patton Boyle, *The Desegregated Heart* (New York: William Morrow and Co., 1962) 75.
[2] Ibid., 84.
[3] Ibid., 88.

undertook an extended re-education in "The T. J. Sellers Course for Backward Southerners." By May 1951, after a year of agonizing reappraisal of her intellectual and moral attitudes, Mrs. Boyle reached the point where she had to make a pivotal decision: would she press on with her "integration" crusade? "I made the decision on a Friday night and all day Saturday I was sick within. The Southern Code muttered in my ear through the day into the night. I no longer believed in it but I could still hear its voice...I was haunted by the feeling that I was being catapulted into outer space, far from all that I had known. Next day when I went to church, conscious fear so surrounded me with chill, stiff hands that my fingers were clumsy as I sought in my hymnal the number posted for the processional. It was #536. I sang it mechanically until I reached the last stanza. Then I felt suddenly eased:

'Earth shall be fair, and all her people one:
Nor till that hour shall God's whole will be done.
Now, even now, once more from earth to sky
Peals forth in joy man's old, undaunted cry,
"Earth shall be fair, and all her folk be one"'[4]

In the next three months, she drafted enough liberal friends to join her in publishing fifty-one letters in the leading Virginia newspapers supporting integration. Still the Editor of the *Richmond Times-Dispatch*, Virginius Dabney, cautioned her, "The less said about it the better," and being the die-hard that he was, he refused to publish hers. She barged ahead, becoming active in the NAACP and the newly rejuvenated Virginia Council of Human Relations. She wrote a regular column in the weekly Negro newspaper, *The Tribune*. In December 1952, she managed to get an

---

[4] Ibid., 123.

article in the national journal, *The Christian Century*. But she was learning the hard way. "With immutable justice I was to learn one day that a whole city full of frank enemies who shout threats and insults cannot tear one's heart out as can one liberal who turns his back on a molested brother in the name of faith in the South."[5] This awareness came upon her, following the Brown decision of the US Supreme Court in 1954, when the Human Relations Council of the state informed her that her voice was no longer needed: "You are identified in the public mind as an extremist."

On 15 November 1954, in response to the Supreme Court's mandate to desegregate the public schools, the Virginia Governor staged a Public Education Hearing. For fourteen long hours, sixty-eight segregationists harangued the audience; only six spoke up for integration, one of those being Mrs. Boyle. When she testified for the NAACP against the state of Virginia, to prove in court that its state law to abolish the organization was unconstitutional, the wrath of the so-called liberals mounted. "One white 'moderate' voiced the opinion which I sensed was widespread but which until then I had heard only from the opposition: 'You don't belong with us; you belong with the Negroes.'"[6] The key event in her rejection was the publication on 15 February 1955 of her article in the *Saturday Evening Post*, entitled "Southerners Will Like Integration." It appeared with an accompanying photograph of Sarah Patton Boyle walking between two black students on the University campus. She immediately saw that both items would be provocative. (Earlier she had argued with the editor to preserve her original title, "We Are Readier Than We Think," but to no avail.) Now the storm of Southern malice rained down upon her. A cross was burned on her lawn: "There it stood below, six feet tall and not a slipper's toss from the house, the flames stretching eastward in

[5] Ibid., 166.
[6] Ibid., 284.

the light breeze like banners of evil. The soft hiss and crackle was a fitting voice for live malice, and the odor of burning, oil-soaked rags a fitting miasma of human moral degradation. Little blasts of dry, scorching air, made soulless by unholy heat, beat in my face. Here was an expression of hate which shocked four senses with the forceful thrust of evil."[7]

When the Martinsville, Virginia, branch of the NAACP requested her to speak about the "personal difficulties that white Virginians encounter when they take a stand for integration," she decided to formalize her feelings. She reminded them that when "the minority member makes an open stand for integration, he has one comfort to sustain him on his difficult road. This is the knowledge that he is giving voice to the official position of his group. He knows that he can count on the approval and moral support of his press, and of all the outstanding leaders and intellects in the colored world....But the white citizen who defends minority rights does not have this comfort. His job is often endangered; his life is sometimes threatened. And discouragement hangs equally heavy on his heart. But unlike his colored brother, he has no hiding place. For his own people are the ones he has chosen to oppose."[8]

---

[7] Ibid., 253.
[8] Ibid., 257.

CHARLES MORGAN

In Birmingham on 15 September 1963 an explosion rocked the Sixteenth Street Baptist Church as the children gathered for Sunday School. The bomb had been thrown against the church by white racists who lacked any restraints of human compassion. The following day an "explosion" disturbed the regular Monday luncheon of the Young Men's Business Club. Charles Morgan, a prominent member, in a speech reacting to the previous day's tragedy, dropped a bombshell in their laps. "A mad, remorseful, worried community asks, 'Who did it' The answer should be, 'We all did it.'"

The church bombing killed four little girls. The civic club speech doomed Charles Morgan and his promising legal career; the city did not literally drum him out of town but they united to make his life, and that of his family, so miserable that within the year he was forced to move away. He had exposed what Martin Luther King's letter three months earlier had labeled "the appalling silence of good people;" he had broken the Southern white code of civility by charging that the rapidly accumulating acts of violence were due to their own racist ideas and behavior. He charged that Birmingham, his home for eighteen years, was "a city where no one accepts responsibility...a leaderless city...(with) a moderate mayor elected to change things (yet) moves so slowly...A governor who offers a reward but mentions not his own failure to preserve law and order...Lawyers and politicians who counsel people as to what the law is not, when they know full well what the law is." He was especially hard on its clergy:

> Birmingham is the only city in America where the police and the sheriff, in the school crisis, had to call our local ministers together to tell them to do their duty. The ministers of Birmingham who have done so little for Christianity call for prayer at high noon in a city of lawlessness.[1]

He spared no one. "But you know the 'who' of 'Who did it?' is really rather simple. The 'who' is every little individual who talks about the 'niggers' and spreads the seeds of his hate to his neighbor and his son. The jokester, the crude oaf whose racial jokes rock the party with laughter. The 'who' is every governor who ever shouted for lawlessness and became a law violator. It is every Senator and every Representative who in the halls of Congress stands and with mock humility tells the world that things back home aren't really like they are. It is courts that move ever so slowly and newspapers that timorously defend the law. It is all the Christians and their ministers who spoke too late in anguished cries against violence. It is the coward in each of us who clucks admonitions...We are a mass of intolerance and bigotry and stand indicted before our young. We are cursed by the failure of each of us to accept responsibility, by our defense of an already dead institution."[2]

Charles Morgan, thirty-three years old, married and with a son, living in a wealthy suburb, with a thriving law practice, had not always shared these views. He had been reared properly to be a true son of the South. He attended the University of Alabama for seven years, earning both undergraduate and law degrees. On campus, he

---

[1] Charles Morgan, *A Time to Speak* (New York: Harper and Row, 1964) 12.
[2] Ibid., 11.

was outstanding, accepted in Omega-Delta-Kappa, recipient of law school honors, and elected to leadership positions. He returned home to establish his own law office and entered fully into the professional circles of the city. He was on the fast track to becoming a top leader of its future. He had been president of the Junior Bar and the local Heart Association; the Advisory Committee on Schools, the State Mental Health Association and he had won the Man of the Year Award. Everything was going his way—so it seemed.

But during the very nine years of his promising law practice he had been encountering cases where basic civil rights were being run over roughshod. His eyes were being opened to the callousness with which his Alabamian peers regarded such violations—cases in which public opinion weighed more heavily than the legal process. His Southern mindset had been troubled at the outset of his legal practice when Autherine Lucy had filed her application in 1955 to enter the University. Later, as a novice lawyer he was obliged to accept pro bono cases for poor blacks caught in the wheels of the courts, and he suddenly discovered how racism effected every stage of the proceedings. However, it was four white litigants over the most recent three years—whose volatile cases somehow ended up in his lap—which raised his ire. Thomas Reeves (1960), Robert Hughes (1960), Norman Jimerson (1962), Bob Zellner (1963). They were all ministers charged with crimes, all the charges stemming from their liberal views on race. Three of them were natives to the region, not "outside agitators," they had trained in local colleges. They were mild people, genuinely dedicated to the precepts of Christ. They could not be classified as "criminals" by a long shot; they were not lawbreakers in the ordinary sense. Yet they were jailed and manhandled in the cruelest manner. In accepting these cases, Morgan knew very well that he was going against the grain, that he would quickly be categorized as "the

lawyer for nigger-lovers," that he would jeopardize his lucrative
law practice, that both his legal associates and the general public
would likely turn their back on him. When he was requested by the
Bar Association to defend the Rev. Robert Hughes, Executive
Director of the Alabama Human Relations Council, who was
refusing a court order to submit complete records of his
organization, Morgan reflected:

> Once again, I had to consider what effect handling a contro-
> versial race relations case might have on my career. There were
> possible economic consequences. And there were bound to be
> political consequences. I knew I had to discuss these matters with
> Camille (his wife). She, too, had an investment in our prac-
> tice...She had persevered through my hectic law school days...she
> had lent encouragement, not to mention long secretarial hours,
> when I decided to leave the corporate firm and strike out on my
> own....Now, with the Hughes case, we might be risking all this
> investment of time and toil; and possibly more, for representing
> Hughes meant frontline involvement on the unpopular side of a
> bitter community controversy. There was the possibility of un-
> pleasant social and personal ramifications, a consideration that
> no family with a child in school can wholly ignore. And lurking
> in the background was the greater unpleasantness of having our
> telephone number added to the hate-mongers' list for nighttime
> calls.[3]

Indeed the negative consequences mounted quickly. The Klan
targeted him with a campaign of telephone calls, threats of
violence, and publicly labeled him the key lawyer for the
integrationists. It was the abandonment of his wide circle of
friends and associates which most hurt. "You've destroyed your
usefulness here" were the words most often put by former friends

---

[3] Ibid., 74-75.

who now remained silent and at a distance. Commenting upon the ostracization of Norman Jimerson, who had taken over Hughes' position after he was forced to leave Alabama, Morgan indirectly refers to his own plight:

> In Norman Jimerson I saw a human being, a good but a misunderstood human being, lose his social moorings. He was not merely cut adrift from the white society of the community, but neither did he have any place in the Negro society for whose cause he had sacrificed himself. The Negro involved in the racial struggle of the Deep South stands with his community. But the white Southerner who champions the Negro cause may be an outsider both on his own and to the Negro community. Once again my enthusiasm for fighting what I knew to be the good fight was chilled by a realization of what happened to those who dared swim against the current of conformity. The age-old fear of ostracism, of being not merely an outsider, but an outcast from your own community, has killed more free spirits than fear of physical harm.[4]

In the long hours, sleepless nights, week on end, Morgan had moved from a detached, expert legal counselor to become a person deeply involved with the conscientious witness of his rare clients.

> The impact of my experiences in the Reeves and Hughes cases fundamentally changed my perspective on the community I called home and toward my role as a Birmingham attorney. I had given up the luxury of detachment from the causes I represented...Now I myself had become involved, not simply as a lawyer but as a member of the community—as a person who had a share of responsibility for the things that were happening in my home and in my city.[5]

[4] Ibid., 132, 134.
[5] Ibid., 83.

All these legal actions and reappraisals were crowding Morgan's mind on the Monday that he made his civic club speech. He was beset with frustrations born of disgust, impatience and disappointment. He spoke his heart and awaited the reactions. "Now, in the community's hour of crisis, it seemed, I had been able to perform a service after all—by providing the scapegoat it needed to survive the weeks and months ahead. If the image had been tarnished, the fault lay not with the community but with its critics. By speaking out, I had done the community a wrong. This was the prevailing sentiment."[6] They no longer had a place for his voice in Birmingham. In departing the city—closing his law office, moving his child out of school, and selling their home—he managed in the book he wrote within the year, A Time to Speak, to provide his own epitaph:

> If Birmingham and cities like it are to have hope, it must come from those members of the white community who are not afraid to succumb to their conscience. There are too few of these people. There always are. But they are there. They go about their business until some circumstance or event, large or small, calls for commitment. For some, this commitment may mean financial, social or political ruin. Some may escape society's more stringent sanctions. Perhaps there will be no retribution. But, when he acts, the Southern white man can never be certain it will not mean his job, or community standing, or his physical safety.[7]

---

[6] Ibid., 166.
[7] Ibid., 168.

ROBERT HUGHES

Robert Hughes was a Methodist minister in Birmingham, Alabama, who had been seconded by the North Alabama Methodist Conference to head the newly formed Alabama Council of Human Relations. This was an affiliate of the Southern Regional Council, headquartered in Atlanta. For several decades, the SRC had operated as a research and publicist organization to promote the progressive views of the South in the general area of education, economics, politics, and race relations. It was never considered a radical organization and had adhered to a policy of accommodationist biracial communications. It did not out-rightly oppose Jim Crow laws until 1949. With the coming of the Brown decision of the U.S. Supreme Court in 1954 and a sizeable grant from the Ford Foundation to assist the SRC to help Southern states to implement that decision, it was instantly rejuvenated. Its membership was composed mostly of moderates, businessmen, ministers, educators, and housewives, both black and white, from the educated middle-class. It established chapters throughout the state, but mostly it operated outside the mainstream of the civic power structures. Under the rubric, "human relations," its membership deliberately refrained from embracing the term "integration"— with some few exceptions. On the other hand, the majority of the whites, all of whom vehemently opposed implementing the Brown decision, interpreted the term "human relations" as a cover for forcing integration down their throats.

Reverend Hughes himself belonged to the Montgomery Improvement Association, formed by Martin Luther King Jr. to lead the bus boycott in Montgomery and King himself belonged to the Montgomery chapter of the Alabama Council on Human Relations. So, if not close friends, they saw each other frequently and considered themselves allies in the cause of integration. That act, along with other such initiatives, was bound to make Hughes a target of the racists at large. For instance, he took the lead in defending a white seminarian, Thomas Reeves, who had publicly opposed the formation of the segregationist Methodist Laymen's Union in 1959. Consequently, the Ku Klux Klan burned a cross in Hughes' yard. He was harassed not only by the local hate sheets, late-night telephone callers, and threats on his wife's life, but the Birmingham Police Department, under orders from Bull Conners pursued a policy of aggressive surveillance of Hughes and other select members of the Alabama Council on Human Relations.

Things reached a boiling point with Harrison Salisbury's lead article in the *New York Times* of 8 April 1960. He concluded his indictment of Birmingham as America's "most racist city," "Every channel of communication, every medium of mutual interest, every reasoned approach, every inch of middle ground has been fragmented by the emotional dynamite of racism." The white leadership of Birmingham was outraged, and immediately began proceedings to sue Salisbury for slander. As part of that legal strategy, Salisbury's telephone records while residing in the city, were subpoenaed and Hughes was identified as his main source of information. The Bessemer grand jury, where Alabama criminal libel laws were being tested in the Salisbury case, had a subpoena duces tecum served on Hughes to appear before it on 1 September 1960. He had to appear within forty-eight hours, bringing with him "all records, books, cancelled checks, memorandums, letters, correspondence showing all contributions and donations made to Robert E. Hughes, or the Alabama Council on Human Relations, during the period from 1 January 1958, to the present date..." Hughes was quite willing to appear in his own person, but he felt that the order for his organization's records made the Council itself the target. Compliance would jeopardize individual careers of the members exposed and might well destroy the last remaining bi-racial group in the state. He decided to fight the grand jury's subpoena through the courts and somehow managed to secure the services of Birmingham's one civil rights lawyer, Charles Morgan. "What do you think will happen?" Hughes asked his lawyer on the way to the Bessemer courthouse. "That's for the court and the Lord to decide, Bob. I'll do my best in court. The Lord is your jurisdiction."[1] All of Morgan's successive motions to quash the proceedings were denied over the next two days, and at the end of the day—2 September—after Hughes had appeared before the grand jury empty-handed, he was adjudged in contempt of court and immediately placed in jail. Hughes spent a long Labor Day weekend in jail. Meanwhile, white moderates within the state were horrified that the Council leader, a respected Methodist minister, was lodged in jail, and statewide pressure was mounted to have Hughes released. Even persons who disagreed with his views were embarrassed by this turn of events. On Tuesday, he was suddenly brought out of jail, where, in the lobby, the sheriff handed him a piece of paper. It was another subpoena, but this time, remarkably, there was no request for organization records. He immediately went before the grand jury empty-handed; the grand jury decided not to pursue the Hughes matter any further.

His secular ordeal was over, but his own ecclesiastical support group, the Methodist Conference to which he belonged, were

---

[1] Charles Morgan, *A Time to Speak* (New York: Harper and Row, 1964) 77.

decidedly not happy with his "integrationist" stance. They ordered him to either resign his position as Executive Director of the Human Relations Council and accept a new assignment or be dismissed from the ministry. For two days, he was stripped of his clergy-status, but, in the mysterious ways of "Christian politics," he was suddenly granted his original missionary goal, to serve in Africa. (He later wrote that the racial tensions he encountered on the mission field of Southern Rhodesia—now Zimbabwe—were not unlike those he had left in Alabama.) Hughes left a letter that gives a glimpse into his mood during the whole embarrassing affair: "I remember so well driving home alone the afternoon I was removed from the ministry. Passing through the South-side Negro area I passed a small Negro boy, eight or nine years old, walking along the gutter kicking a tin can aimlessly. I caught a glimpse of his dejected face in the gathering dusk and the thought struck me that what I had done might have, by a small degree, made his future brighter. For some reason, I suddenly realized that the opposition didn't really matter—the acceptance or rejection of others was not really as important as whether or not I had done my best. Certainly we are called upon to be faithful before we are called upon to be effective."[2]

---

[2] Ibid., 85.

GEORGE WILLIAMSON

Today George Williamson is pastor of the First Baptist Church in Granville, Ohio. But on 23 February 1960 he was a junior enrolled in Wake Forest University. On the campus, he was quite popular, involved in fraternity life, campus politics and sports, in other words a BMOC (big man on the campus). He was also a ministerial student who took his Baptist youth training in Atlanta, Georgia seriously. He may have heard of Thoreau and Gandhi in his classes—he was a philosophy major—but they scarcely caused a ripple in his thinking. On this particular day, the last thing in his mind was going to jail. But that's exactly what happened.

The sit-in movement had just begun in the nearby city of Greensboro, North Carolina. Now some of the black students at the local Winston Salem State University were planning to follow suit at the lunch counter of the downtown dime store. As he reflected on his state of mind prior to that day, he says:

> Up until that point I had nothing but negative reaction to anything connected with the Civil Rights Movement; certainly my attitudes toward Martin Luther King were extremely negative, and whatever I knew about the movement I thought of in pretty much the same terms that everybody in my culture was describing them. It was disruptive. It was demagogic. There was no point in it other than the ego of a few individual leaders, and

it was leading to chaos in Southern culture. It was turning black people and white people against each other, and in my simple minded view I thought black people and white people got along fine. All my family and friends looked upon King as a communist and I felt the same way."

So far as I remember, I didn't know the term 'civil disobedience.' I hadn't read Thoreau. I didn't understand that about King. I just thought of him as a criminal. Anybody who's arrested is a criminal—that's the end of it. Police are good, criminals are bad. Laws are good, lawless people are bad—that's the whole of it. Of course, I knew the Bible as a child and a young person. All that stuff in the prophets about justice, I thought that meant criminals getting what they were due—spending time in jail for being bad."[1]

Nonetheless, on that day in February, Williamson and several other Wake Forest students decided to investigate what was happening with their peers from the neighboring institution.

They knew none of the black students personally. They connected by phone and agreed to meet at a certain point downtown. "Meeting them was a kind of life-transforming experience for me. I'd known scores and scores of black people, all my life, but I'd never met a peer. Those were all servants and people in low class jobs, so this was my first experience of somebody who's like me. Everything about them was just like myself, except that they were black. So we walked together into Woolworth's. As soon as we entered, they surrounded us, blocking our way to the lunch counter, and immediately the police came. They told us we could either leave or be arrested. So far as I know, I hadn't really seriously considered arrest up until that point, even though we knew the students in Greensboro had been arrested.

---

[1] This quotation and all subsequent quotations are taken from G. McLeod Bryan, *Making History* (Wake Forest University Printing Office, 1999), 18 pages.

About half of our group left—white kids, that is. Of course, none of the black kids left. Probably all of them had been arrested a lot in their lives, just being black; so arrest wasn't any big deal to them. But, as I later learned, arrest meant a great deal more to them than that. It was their moral stand. For me, I didn't mean to be arrested, but I just kind of froze. I couldn't move. So I was arrested more de facto than by intention. Then the paddy wagons drove up and they loaded the ten of us white students along with all the blacks and carried us to jail. In the jail we were immediately segregated, the blacks in one part and we whites in the other. My neat, safe, happy, promising world was abruptly turned up-side-down. It dawned upon me that I was labeled forever."

"The one thing in my life that changed me more than anything else was getting arrested. There was a big curtain that dropped on my life, and everything before that was one life, and everything after that was another life. Overnight I was a traitor to my people. I was the enemy, there was no foothold anywhere. Everybody thought I was bad, thought I was evil, thought I was sick. A nigger-lover! That's a sick thing."

Their subsequent trial only added insult to injury. Somehow the prosecutor had pried over the week into their past lives and learned that two of the Wake Forest students had traveled in Europe the summer before, traveled together unmarried. The only "indicted criminal" he placed in the docket for questioning was the young lady, Margaret Dutton. Quizzing her ruthlessly about her previous summer, he finally got around to asking about her visit in Vienna. "Did you go to the Spanish Riding School? Did you see the Castle? And what else did you visit?...Did you by chance attend the World Youth Festival that was convening in Vienna at the time you were there" With some hesitation, Margaret answered in the affirmative. (Now that festival was known to have been sponsored by communist nations; so the prosecutor had made his point loud and clear.) There was no further questioning and with that brief exchange, the ten Wake Forest students were sentenced for trespassing, but more significantly condemned in the public eye as being motivated by communist sympathies.

Williamson also learned that overnight all his old dependable alliances had abandoned him because of his civil rights stand—gone were the Baptists, his fraternity brothers, and even his Wake Forest administration, trustees, and faculty (for the most part) support. The President summoned all ten of them after the trial to the Board of Trustees Room next to his office. He addressed them in the following manner ("dressed them down" would be a better expression): "Now you've made your point, but it's not what students are about. So why don't you go back to your rooms, attend classes and be good students." (Be quiet and don't become involved in the greatest moral movement to hit the campuses of America in the twentieth century.) He concluded by asking for any comments. One of the ten students, who seemed to be the weakest of the group of protesters, jumped to his feet. "Dr. Tribble, if you're trying to tell me to shut up and put up, I want to tell you something...We have just been treated unjustly by an unjust judicial system. We were falsely accused of being communist, and sentenced on that spurious charge. I was reared on the civic book morality where this sort of thing is not supposed to happen in American democracy. We broke laws that were wrong because God told us to break those laws. Now you expect me to be quiet...No! The rest of my life I'm going to spend trying to rectify this mess."

Indeed, George Williamson has joined that student in working for social justice in America for the last forty years.

TOM HOLMES

Following the collapse of his pastoral ministry at the Tattnall Square Baptist Church, situated on Mercer University campus in Macon, Georgia, the Reverend Tom Holmes reflects on the harsh reality which led to his dismissal in his autobiography, *Ashes for Breakfast*:

> It is difficult for the average American to realize how strong the Southern racial mystique is. It has been nurtured for more than 150 years. It is as deeply ingrained in Southerners as their basic Protestant character. As a matter of fact, the two have become so intertwined in Southern minds and hearts that an attack on one produces a Pavlovian response from the other. In Georgia, where politics is always a major interest, especially with its racial overtones, the reasoned approach is scorned and candidates are forced to deal almost exclusively with the so-called 'gut issue.' It is foolhardy for a Southern minister to believe that a great many of his church leaders are going to take any action that appears 'unpatriotic' to the Southern mind or 'communistic inspired' during a political campaign. I knew all this, but being an optimist, I would not easily accept the fact.[1]

---

[1] Tom Holmes, *Ashes for Breakfast* (Valley Forge, Pa.: Judson Press, 1960) 71.

One day he had been the popular pastor of a large city church—at differing times sheltering the mayor of the city, ranking police officers, the city attorney, and of course many faculty members and students from the adjoining campus. The next day he was angrily accused by one of his deacons as being "lower down than any dog." What brought about this abrupt change was Pastor Holmes' decision to welcome to his Sunday morning congregation in the spring of 1966 a black person. But Sam Oni was an unusual black. He had come from Nigeria where many Mercer graduates had been called to "mission to Africans:" now the very church which sanctioned and financed these missionaries refused to shelter one of their converts. Holmes grieved over the moral contradiction and decided to do something about it. He took the leadership in welcoming Sam Oni into their Christian fellowship. At the deacons' meeting, the week before the Sunday vote of the congregation to oust him from the pastorate, 25 September 1966, he had declared, "My conscience belongs to God, and a thousand votes by the church would not bind it."[2]

That decision had not come easily. One month earlier, someone knocked on his study door. "[This friend] told me that he was a personal friend of two of the FBI agents here in the city. One of them had called him and asked him to warn me of rumors that the Klansmen were talking about some sort of demonstration against me. They could not say what it was or when it would occur, but I was to be on my guard." I was not surprised at the Klan's interest. They were strong in the Macon area, and I had made several comments about the Klan in my morning sermons. This was not the first time in my life I had been warned of possible violence at the hands of hooded nightriders. Without boasting, I was not frightened by this warning. I have always felt that most Klansmen are basically cowards. Their operations are aimed at

---

[2] Ibid.

intimidation and usually are against helpless people, or those they believe will have no way to fight back." "If two of the deacons were Klansmen, I felt they would see to it that the parsonage was not bombed, because it was owned by the church. However, I considered cross-burning on our lawn a possibility....As it turned out, a Klan lynching was not in the cards for the ministers of Tattnall Square Baptist Church. Rather this was to be a 'due process' execution by fellow officials and members of the church."[3]

During the prolonged weeks of turmoil preceding his ouster, certain members pressed him to reconsider his stance. One deacon confided, "Tom, you can solve this problem if you want to. Our people don't want you to leave. You can bring our church together if you will preach just one sermon. Just one sermon will do the trick." "And what would that sermon be," I asked.

He replied:

> "I don't have to tell you. You know," he answered. Yes, I knew what it would be—an admission of error to my basic position and a public statement that I had erred. This would end the confrontation and probably relieve most of the tension. This would 'save the church.' Perhaps I would then be considered a wise administrator. But, having done that, the only course left to me would be the preaching of bland sermons and the avoidance of any attempt to develop a relevant ministry. This would simply be a marking of time. For who can follow a minister who has denied his conscience, lost his self-respect, and ultimately will lose the respect of his friends and enemies.[4]

On October 2, after the September debacle, Sam Oni was again denied admission to enter the morning worship service. He was greeted by an off-duty policeman, a deacon of the church, who

---

[3] Ibid., 73-74.
[4] Ibid., 64.

barred his entrance. The African then proceeded to "preach his sermon," a scene and message carried on national television. In a media interview later, he summed up his position: "I feel that the actions of churches like this repudiate everything that dedicated Christian missionaries are doing." Agreeing with Oni's moral judgment and acting in his behalf cost Tom Holmes his job—but it may have saved his soul.

CONCLUSION

Having read this far, the reader is most likely doubly appalled: appalled at the vicious physical and psychological abuse inflicted by the majority of white southerners on their white compatriots who sided with their Black brothers and sisters in the Freedom Movement and appalled that so few white southerners joined the ranks of the protesters against racism. More importantly, the reader may ask himself or herself, where would I have stood in those days? A corollary question may also rush to consciousness: were some of the people in these howling mobs and among the government officials standing adamant defending Jim Crow laws and customs my neighbors and friends perhaps my kinspeople, yes, even my grandparents and parents? Yes, even my fellow church members. One must remember that it was exactly during these days that virtually every First Baptist Church in every metropolitan center of the south locked its doors to prevent Blacks from their worship services and passed laws within their membership to keep Blacks from joining – that from the largest Christian denomination in the Southland. And , as John Lewis has reminded us in this recent autobiography chronicling his beginnings in the Civil Rights Movement from the time he was a student in the American Baptist Theological School in Nashville, Tennessee, the students' major obstacle was the President of that school whose salary was paid in part by the Southern Baptist Convention.

All of these facts make clear that a heavy cloud of cultural complicity in the events profiled in this book still hangs over the racial complexity of the Twenty-first Century. As Professor Alton Pollard reminds us in the Foreword, a major task of reconciliation, rehabilitation, and renewal still lies ahead for the American nation. Unfortunately, unlike South Africa within the past decade, our nation has not had a Truth and Reconciliation Committee where the perpetrators of torture and death must confront their victims and be forced to confess and ask for forgiveness. A sweeping one-time confession of sin on the part of the white culture is not sufficient. That's too much like window-dressing to make outsiders believe that everything within the household of democracy is okay. Instead, our nation must come face-to-face with its shody record of racism: from its very start in the mistreatment of the native American population down to the present moment of politically maneuvered "fixes."

Some social psychologists have suggested that social revolutions originate with the citizens who are marginalized. That opinion may explain in part the spontaneous rising of the American Black in the Freedom Movement in which tens of thousands were willing to suffer and to go to prison for their rights. But it does not explain the few southern whites that prompted this book. More often than not these persons were from the middle or upper class; they risked losing their careers, their families, their friends, their secure and comfortable worlds built upon exploitation of their Black under-lings.

Again, much credit has been given to students for their majority role in the Civil Rights Movement. Students, the historians argue, could lead because they had so little to lose: no vested jobs, careers, social roles, financial stake, or families. Yet only seven of the thirty-one persons profiled were students; the majority had everything to lose yet still risked it all.

But, perhaps, the most significant trait they shared was the social paradox that they derived their strength from the very cultural milieu which rejected them. In other words, they cannot be charged with "having their minds messed up," as the locals put it, by living outside their native Southland. Somehow they were able to tap the submerged resources of their Bible Belt region and transform it into a wider humanitarian perspective. Somehow they were able to transcend the tragic dimension of southern culture—manifest in the contrast between its ideal myths and the harsh reality of its treatment of blacks, of women, and of "outsiders." (This contradiction has been vividly depicted in W. J. Cash's classic study, *The Mind of the South*, in 1941, but few Southerners had awakened to it at the time.)

Finally, the question still remains: why did they do what they did? As one who has studied their witness for decades, I have no easy or simple answer. In this book, I have merely provided them a platform for their personal testimonies. There are certainly some predominant motifs that run throughout their stories, but my purpose as an author is to allow the reader to ponder these testimonies in order that she or he may derive some guidance for the direction their own lives may take in their day of decision-making on the question of racism.